Louis Untermeyer has compiled ten
poetry anthologies, widely used
as textbooks, and has translated
Heine, Horace, and Ernst Toller.
During the war he was with the
OWI and has since done free-lance
editorial work for many publishers.

A GENUINE POCKET BOOK ANTHOLOGY...

# THE POCKET BOOK OF

# AMERICAN POEMS

## From the Colonial Period to the Present Day

≈ EDITED AND WITH AN INTRODUCTION BY ≈
## LOUIS UNTERMEYER

POCKET BOOKS, INC. • ROCKEFELLER CENTER, N.Y.

The Printing History of

THE POCKET BOOK OF AMERICAN POEMS

POCKET BOOK edition published September, 1948
1st printing....................August, 1948

This original edition, prepared especially for
POCKET BOOKS, INC., is printed from brand-new
plates made from newly set, large, clear, easy-
to-read type.

## ACKNOWLEDGMENTS

For material copyrighted by authors, publishers, and agents, the editor
of THE POCKET BOOK OF AMERICAN POEMS is indebted to the following:

BRANDT & BRANDT, for permission to reprint "The Quarrel" by Conrad
Aiken, from *John Deth and Other Poems*, published by Charles Scribner's
Sons, copyright, 1929, by Conrad Aiken; "American Names" from *Selected
Works of Stephen Vincent Benet*, published by Rinehart & Company, Inc.,
copyright, 1927, by Stephen Vincent Benet; "Nightmare #3" from *Selected
Works of Stephen Vincent Benet*, published by Rinehart & Company, Inc.,
copyright, 1935, by Stephen Vincent Benet; "Pity Me Not" by Edna St.
Vincent Millay, from *The Harp-Weaver and Other Poems*, published by
Harper & Brothers, copyright, 1920, by Edna St. Vincent Millay; "Dirge
Without Music" by Edna St. Vincent Millay, from *The Buck in the Snow*,
published by Harper & Brothers, copyright, 1928, by Edna St. Vincent Millay;
"somewhere i have never travelled, gladly beyond" by E. E. Cummings,
from *Collected Poems*, published by Harcourt, Brace & Co., Inc., copyright,
1931, by E. E. Cummings.

# ACKNOWLEDGMENTS (*continued*)

Curtis Brown, Ltd., for permission to reprint for the British Empire, except Canada, and the territory outside the United States and the British Empire "Boy With His Hair Cut Short" by Muriel Rukeyser, from *U. S. 1*, published by The Viking Press, copyright, 1938, by Muriel Rukeyser. Reprinted by permission of the author.

Jonathan Cape, Ltd. and the Executors of Emily Dickinson, for permission to reprint for the British Empire, except Canada, "The Wind Took up the Northern Things", "The Mountains Stood in Haze", and "I Thought the Train Would Never Come" by Emily Dickinson, from *Bolts of Melody*.

The John Day Company, Inc., for permission to reprint "Sundown" from *The High Falcon* by Léonie Adams, copyright by Léonie Adams, October 10, 1929.

Dodd, Mead & Company, for permission to reprint "The Fawn in the Snow" from *Golden Fleece* by William Rose Benet, copyright, 1933, by Dodd, Mead & Company, Inc.

Doubleday & Company, for permission to reprint "Poets to Come", "I Hear America Singing", "Song of Myself", "On The Beach at Night", "When Lilacs Last in the Dooryard Bloom'd", "O Captain! My Captain!", "Dirge For Two Veterans", "By Blue Ontario's Shore", "Give Me The Splendid Silent Sun", "To A Locomotive in Winter", "When I Heard The Learned Astronomer", and "The Last Invocation" from *Leaves of Grass* by Walt Whitman, copyright, 1924, by Doubleday & Company, Inc.

Eyre & Spottiswoode, Ltd., for permission to reprint "Bells for John Whiteside's Daughter" from John Crowe Ransom's *Selected Poems* for sale in the British Empire, except Canada.

Faber & Faber, Ltd., for permission to reprint "The Fish" from *Selected Poems* by Marianne Moore in *The Pocket Book of American Poems* for sale in the British Empire, except Canada, and open market.

Harcourt, Brace and Company, Inc., for permission to reprint "Upstream" from *Slabs of The Sunburnt West* by Carl Sandburg, copyright, 1922, by Harcourt, Brace and Company, Inc.; "Ask No Return" from *Poems 1930-1940* by Horace Gregory, copyright, 1930, 1933, 1935, 1941, by Horace Gregory; "Warning to One" from *The Noise That Time Makes* by Merrill Moore, copyright, 1929, by Harcourt, Brace and Company, Inc.; "Mary Winslow" from *Lord Weary's Castle* by Robert Lowell, copyright, 1944, 1946, by Robert Lowell.

Harper & Brothers, for permission to reprint in the United States, Canada, and the world outside the British Empire "The Wind Took Up The Northern Things", "The Mountains Stood in Haze", and "I Thought the Train Would Never Come" by Emily Dickinson from *Bolts of Melody, New Poems of Emily Dickinson*, Edited by Mabel Loomis Todd and Millicent Todd Bingham, published by Harper & Brothers, copyright, 1945, by Millicent Todd Bingham.

Henry Holt and Company, Inc., for permission to reprint "Mowing", "The Death of the Hired Man", "The Telephone" and "The Runaway" from *Collected Poems of Robert Frost*, 1939, copyright, 1930, 1939, by Henry Holt and Company, Inc., copyright, 1936, by Robert Frost; "Hyla Brook" and "Choose Something Like a Star" from *Come In and Other Poems* by Robert Frost, copyright, 1943, by Henry Holt and Company, Inc.; "Prayers of Steel" from *Cornhuskers* by Carl Sandburg, copyright, 1918, by Henry Holt and Company.

Houghton Mifflin Company, for permission to reprint "Madonna of the Evening Flowers" by Amy Lowell, and "You, Andrew Marvell" and "The End of the World" by Archibald MacLeish.

# ACKNOWLEDGMENTS (*continued*)

ALFRED A. KNOPF, INC., for permission to reprint "To the One of Fictive Music" from *Harmonium* by Wallace Stevens, copyright, 1923, 1931, by Alfred A. Knopf, Inc.; "The Winter Sleep" from *Collected Poems of Elinor Wylie*, copyright, 1921, 1932, by Alfred A. Knopf, Inc.; "Bells for John Whiteside's Daughter" from *Selected Poems* by John Crowe Ransom, copyright, 1924, 1945, by Alfred A. Knopf, Inc.

LITTLE, BROWN & COMPANY, for permission to reprint "I'm Nobody! Who are You?", "Of All the Souls that Stand Create", "I Never Saw a Moor", "Elysium Is as Far", "Because I Could not Stop for Death", "I Taste a Liquor Never Brewed", "Hope Is the Thing with Feathers", "I Dreaded that First Robin So", "There Came a Day at Summer's Full", "Success is Counted Sweetest" and "I Had Been Hungry all the Years" from *Poems by Emily Dickinson*, edited by Martha Dickinson Bianchi and Alfred Leete Hampson.

LIVERIGHT PUBLISHING CORPORATION, for permission to reprint "The Garden" and "Lethe" from *Collected Poems by "H. D."*, and "Voyages: II" from *Poems* by Hart Crane.

THE MACMILLAN COMPANY, for permission to reprint in the United States and Canada "Eros Turannos" from *The Man Against The Sky* by Edwin Arlington Robinson, copyright, 1916, by The Macmillan Company, and "The Fish" by Marianne Moore from *Selected Poems*, copyright, 1935, by Marianne Moore; "The Eagle that is Forgotten" from *General Wm. Booth Enters Heaven & Other Poems* by Vachel Lindsay, copyright, 1913, by The Macmillan Company; "The Broncho that Would not be Broken" from *The Chinese Nightingale & Other Poems* by Vachel Lindsay, copyright, 1917, by The Macmillan Company; "Wisdom" from *Dark of the Moon* by Sara Teasdale, copyright, 1926, by The Macmillan Company; "Let it be Forgotten" from *Flame and Shadow* by Sara Teasdale, copyright, 1920, by The Macmillan Company.

MACMILLAN & CO., LTD., for permission to reprint "Eros Turannos" by Edwin Arlington Robinson in *The Pocket Book of American Poems* for sale outside the United States and Canada.

VIRGIL MARKHAM, for permission to reprint "Lincoln, the Man of the People" and "The Man With the Hoe" by Edwin Markham.

MARTIN SECKER & WARBURG, LTD., for permission to reprint "The Leg" from *V-Letter and Other Poems* by Karl Shapiro in the British Empire, except Canada.

RANDOM HOUSE, for permission to reprint "Hurt Hawks" by Robinson Jeffers, copyright, 1929, by Robinson Jeffers.

REYNAL AND HITCHCOCK, INC., for permission to reprint "The Leg" from *V-Letter and Other Poems* by Karl Shapiro in the United States, Canada, and open market.

CHARLES SCRIBNER'S SONS, for permission to reprint "The Marshes of Glynn" from *Poems* by Sidney Lanier; "Triumph of Love" from *Poems, 1911-1936* by John Hall Wheelock, copyright, 1936, by Charles Scribner's Sons; "Uncle Ananias" and "The Master" from *The Town Down The River* by Edwin Arlington Robinson, copyright, 1910, by Charles Scribner's Sons, 1938, by Ruth Niveson; "Credo" from *Children of the Night* by Edwin Arlington Robinson.

THE VIKING PRESS, INC., for permission to reprint "Autumn" from *Love and Need: Collected Poems* by Jean Starr Untermeyer, copyright, 1918, by B. W. Huebsch, 1946, by Jean Starr Untermeyer; "Boy With His Hair Cut Short" from *U. S. 1*, by Muriel Rukeyser for sale in the United States and Canada, copyright, 1938, by Muriel Rukeyser.

# CONTENTS

# CONTENTS

# AN INTRODUCTION

No collection of poetry, no matter how large or how inclusive, can call itself complete. There will never be space enough for all the poets of any period; there will always be readers ready to detect and quick to resent the omission of their favorite, no matter how obscure or unimportant he may be.

This anthology is no exception. It does not pretend to include nearly all the poets who ever published a volume in these states. It does, however, offer a variegated panorama of American poetry. Within its limits it explores a wide terrain and reveals not only the growth but the range and richness of the native spirit. The very differences of subject and manner emphasize the distinctly indigenous nature of this collection.

It may be objected that all the poems in this volume are not of equal merit and that several fall far short of perfection. The objection is valid. A nation's poetry does not consist solely of masterpieces, and an assembly which contained only the most exalted or rarefied examples would be so exclusive and precious as to be unrepresentative. Like most compilations, these pages are a series of compromises between one man's taste and the approval of the many.

Nevertheless, this selection claims to be a representative showing not only of what is best, but what is most characteristic in American verse from the Colonial period to our own times. Without attempting to be a literary history, it acts as a commentary on changing fashions in verse, from the placid eighteenth century imitations to the contemporary experiments in new directions. The confident affirmations of Stephen Vincent Benét are high-lighted against the troubled searching and final serenity of Ralph Waldo Emerson. The loosely rhythmical free verse of Carl Sandburg is anticipated by the long tidal rhythms of Walt Whitman. The modern bucolics of Robert Frost complement and extend the pastoral notes of Bryant and Whittier. The sharp figures of Elinor Wylie and Marianne Moore are pointed by the brilliantly articulated lines of Emily Dickinson, lines which are not only daring in language and breath-taking in imagery, but increasingly penetrating in wisdom.

It is this relation and development which has strengthened American poetry, and it is the constant—one might almost say consistent—variety which has vitalized it. This book reflects the ever-varying contrasts. It emphasizes no one tendency, trend or school; it presents the experimental side by side with the traditional. There is variety even within the groups of poems by the individual authors, contrasting the favorite poems with those poems which have not yet received popular acclaim. Several widely known poems, such as Poe's "The Raven" and Longfellow's "The Children's Hour," have been omitted, chiefly because they have been reprinted so often. Other poems omitted may be found in other volumes published by POCKET BOOKS, INC., especially *The Pocket Book of Verse, The Pocket Reader, The Pocket Companion, The Pocket Treasury, The Pocket Book of Story Poems, The Pocket Book of Popular Verse, The Stephen Vincent Benét Pocket Book,* and *The Pocket Book of Robert Frost's Poems.* A few poems were left out because their length or difficulty did not fit the design of this volume. But, in the main, this compilation attempts to serve two purposes: to give a comprehensive survey of notable achievements in American poetry; and to stimulate, rather than fully satisfy, the reader's further interest in its lowly backgrounds as well as its eminences.

—Louis Untermeyer

*Editor's Note:* Several of the poems in this volume have not previously appeared in an anthology. Unless my search has not been sufficiently thorough, John Quincy Adams' sonnet "To the Sun-Dial" has never been reprinted since its appearance in his forgotten *Poems of Religion and Society,* published in Auburn, New York, in 1850; Freneau's charming genre piece, "On Observing a Large Red-streak Apple," was only recently recovered by Lewis Leary in his *The Last Poems of Philip Freneau* (Rutgers University Press: 1945); and John Saffin's love-lyric "To Her, Coming Home," written in 1654, has remained unknown until 1928 when the late Caroline Hazard brought out *John Saffin His Book* and unearthed a considerable body of neglected poetry. My other indebtednesses are implicit in the following pages.

—L. U.

*Publisher's Note:* Although many critics consider T. S. Eliot an English poet, Mr. Untermeyer had planned to reprint certain poems by Mr. Eliot in this collection of American verse. It is to be regretted that it has been impossible to come to an arrangement with Mr. Eliot's publishers which would have permitted the inclusion.

THE POCKET BOOK OF

# AMERICAN POEMS

# ANNE BRADSTREET                    1612(?)–1672

## From *Contemplations*

When I behold the heavens as in their prime,
  And then the earth, though old, still clad in green,
The stones and trees insensible of time,
  Nor age nor wrinkle on their front are seen;
If winter come, and greenness then doth fade,
A spring returns, and they're more youthful made.
But man grows old, lies down, remains where once he's laid.

By birth more noble than those creatures all,
  Yet seems by nature and by custom cursed—
No sooner born but grief and care make fall
  That state obliterate he had at first;
Nor youth, nor strength, nor wisdom spring again,
Nor habitations long their names retain,
But in oblivion to the final day remain. .

Shall I then praise the heavens, the trees, the earth,
  Because their beauty and their strength last longer?
Shall I wish there or never to had birth,
  Because they're bigger and their bodies stronger?
Nay, they shall darken, perish, fade, and die,
And when unmade so ever shall they lie;
But man was made for endless immortality.

---

The Mariner that on smooth waves doth glide
  Sings merrily and steers his barque with ease,

As if he had command of wind and tide,
  And now become great master of the seas;
But suddenly a storm spoils all the sport,
And makes him long for a more quiet port,
Which 'gainst all adverse winds may serve for fort.

So he that saileth in this world of pleasure,
  Feeding on sweets, that never bit of th' sour,
That's full of friends, of honor, and of treasure,
  Fond fool, he takes this earth ev'n for heav'ns bower.
But sad affliction comes and makes him see
Here's neither honor, wealth, nor safety:
Only above is found all with security.

O Time, the fatal wrack of mortal things,
  That draws oblivion's curtains over kings,
Their sumptuous monuments, men know them not,
  Their names without a record are forgot,
Their parts, their ports, their pomps all laid in th' dust,
Nor wit nor gold nor buildings 'scape time's rust:
But he whose name is grav'd in the white stone
Shall last and shine when all of these are gone.


JOHN SAFFIN                                    1632–1710

### To Her, Coming Home

  Sail, gentle pinnace, Zepherus doth not fail
  With prosperous gales. Sail, gentle pinnace, sail.
  Proud Neptune stoops and freely condescends,
  For's former roughness, now to make amends.
  Thetis with her green mantle sweetly glides
  With smiling dimples, singing by our sides.
  Sail, gentle pinnace, Zepherus doth not fail
  With prosperous gales. Sail, gentle pinnace, sail!

BENJAMIN THOMPSON                    1642–1714

## The Good Old Times

FROM "NEW ENGLAND'S CRISIS"

The times wherein old Pompion was a saint,
When men fared hardly yet without complaint,
On vilest cates; the dainty Indian maize
Was eat with clam-shells out of wooden trays,
Under thatch'd huts without the cry of rent,
And the best sauce to every dish, content.
When flesh was food and hairy skins made coats,
And men as well as birds had chirping notes. . . .
Of Ceres' bounty form'd was many a knack.
Enough to fill poor Robin's Almanac.
These golden times (too fortunate to hold)
Were quickly sinned away for love of gold.
'Twas then among the bushes, not the street,
If one in place did an inferior meet,
"Good-morrow, brother, is there aught you want?
Take freely of me, what I have you ha'nt."
Plain Tom and Dick would pass as current now,
As ever since "Your Servant, Sir," and bow.
Deep-skirted doublets, puritanic capes,
Which now would render men like upright apes,
Was comelier wear, our wiser fathers thought,
Than the cast fashions from all Europe brought.
'Twas in those days an honest grace would hold
Till a hot pudding grew at heart a cold.
And men had better stomachs at religion
Than I to capon, turkey-cock, or pigeon;
When honest sisters met to pray, not prate,
About their own and not their neighbor's state.
During Plain Dealing's reign, that worthy stud
Of the ancient planter's race before the flood,

Then times were good, merchants car'd not a rush
For other fare than Jonakin and Mush.
Although men far'd and lodg'd very hard,
Yet innocence was better than a guard.


EDWARD TAYLOR                    1644(?)–1729

*Upon What Base Was Fixed the Lath Wherein*

Upon what base was fixed the lath wherein
He turned this glove and riggalled it so trim?
Who blew the bellows of His furnace vast?
Or held the mould wherein the world was cast?
Who laid its corner-stone? Or whose commands?
Where stand the pillars upon which it stands?
Who laced and filleted the earth so fine
With rivers like green ribbons smaragdine?
Who made the seas its selvage, and its locks
Like a quilt ball within a silver box?
Who spread its canopy? Or curtains spun?
Who in this bowling alley bowled the sun?


*Housewifery*

Make me, O Lord, Thy spinning-wheel complete.
    Thy holy Word my distaff make for me;
Make mine affections Thy swift flyers neat;
    And make my soul Thy holy spool to be;
    My conversation make to by Thy reel,
    And reel the yarn thereon spun of Thy wheel.

Make me Thy loom then; knit therein this twine;
    And make Thy Holy Spirit, Lord, wind quills.
Then weave the web Thyself. The yarn is fine.

Thine ordinances make my fulling mills.
Then dye the same in heavenly colors choice,
All pinked with varnished flowers of paradise.

Then clothe therewith mine understanding will,
Affections, judgment, conscience, memory,
My words and actions, that their shine may fill
My ways with glory and Thee glorify.
Then mine apparel shall display before Ye
That I am clothed in holy robes for glory.

FRANCIS HOPKINSON                          1737–1791

### The Battle of the Kegs

Gallants attend and hear a friend
    Trill forth harmonious ditty,
Strange things I'll tell which late befell
    In Philadelphia city.

'Twas early day, as poets say,
    Just when the sun was rising,
A soldier stood on a log of wood,
    And saw a thing surprising.

As in amaze he stood to gaze,
    The truth can't be denied, sir,
He spied a score of kegs or more
    Come floating down the tide, sir.

A sailor too in jerkin blue,
    This strange appearance viewing,
First damned his eyes, in great surprise,
    Then said, "Some mischief's brewing.

"These kegs, I'm told, the rebels hold,
    Packed up like pickled herring;
And they're come down to attack the town,
    In this new way of ferrying."

The soldier flew, the sailor too,
    And scared almost to death, sir,
Wore out their shoes, to spread the news,
    And ran till out of breath, sir.

Now up and down throughout the town
    Most frantic scenes were acted;
And some ran here, and others there,
    Like men almost distracted.

Some fire cried, which some denied,
    But said the earth had quakéd;
And girls and boys, with hideous noise,
    Ran through the streets half naked.

Sir William he, snug as a flea,
    Lay all this time a snoring,
Nor dreamed of harm as he lay warm,
    In bed with Mrs. Loring.

Now in a fright, he starts upright,
    Awaked by such a clatter;
He rubs both eyes, and boldly cries,
    "For God's sake, what's the matter?"

At his bedside he then espied,
    Sir Erskine at command, sir,
Upon one foot he had one boot,
    And th'other in his hand, sir.

"Arise, arise," Sir Erskine cries,
　"The rebels—more 's the pity,
Without a boat are all afloat,
　And ranged before the city.


"The motley crew, in vessels new,
　With Satan for their guide, sir,
Packed up in bags, or wooden kegs,
　Come driving down the tide, sir.


"Therefore prepare for bloody war,
　These kegs must all be routed,
Or surely we despised shall be,
　And British courage doubted."


The royal band now ready stand
　All ranged in dread array, sir,
With stomach stout to see it out,
　And make a bloody day, sir.


The cannons roar from shore to shore,
　The small arms make a rattle;
Since wars began I'm sure no man
　E'er saw so strange a battle.


The rebel dales, the rebel vales,
　With rebel trees surrounded,
The distant woods, the hills and floods,
　With rebel echoes sounded.


The fish below swam to and fro,
　Attacked from every quarter;
Why sure, thought they, the devil's to pay,
　'Mongst folks above the water.

The kegs, 'tis said, though strongly made,
    Of rebel staves and hoops, sir,
Could not oppose their powerful foes,
    The conquering British troops, sir.

From morn to night these men of might
    Displayed amazing courage;
And when the sun was fairly down,
    Retired to sup their porridge.

A hundred men with each a pen,
    Or more upon my word, sir,
It is most true would be too few,
    Their valour to record, sir.

Such feats did they perform that day,
    Against these wicked kegs, sir,
That years to come, if they get home,
    They'll make their boasts and brags, sir.

PHILIP FRENEAU                          1752–1832

### The Indian Burying Ground

In spite of all the learned have said,
    I still my old opinion keep;
The posture, that we give the dead,
    Points out the soul's eternal sleep.

Not so the ancients of these lands—
    The Indian, when from life released,
Again is seated with his friends,
    And shares again the joyous feast.

His imaged birds, and painted bowl,
   And venison, for a journey dressed,
Bespeak the nature of the soul,
   Activity, that knows no rest.


His bow, for action ready bent,
   And arrows, with a head of stone,
Can only mean that life is spent,
   And not the old ideas gone.


Thou, stranger, that shalt come this way,
   No fraud upon the dead commit—
Observe the swelling turf, and say
   They do not lie, but here they sit.


Here still a lofty rock remains,
   On which the curious eye may trace
(Now wasted, half, by wearing rains)
   The fancies of a ruder race.


Here still an aged elm aspires,
   Beneath whose far-projecting shade
(And which the shepherd still admires)
   The children of the forest played!


There oft a restless Indian queen
   (Pale Shebah, with her braided hair)
And many a barbarous form is seen
   To chide the man that lingers there.


By midnight moons, o'er moistening dews;
   In habit for the chase arrayed,
The hunter still the deer pursues,
   The hunter and the deer, a shade!

And long shall timorous fancy see
    The painted chief, and pointed spear,
And Reason's self shall bow the knee
    To shadows and delusions here.


### To a Honey Bee

Thou, born to sip the lake or spring,
    Or quaff the waters of the stream,
Why hither come, on vagrant wing?
    Does Bacchus tempting seem—
        Did he for you this glass prepare?
        Will I admit you to a share?


Did storms harass or foes perplex,
    Did wasps or king-birds bring dismay—
Did wars distress, or labors vex,
    Or did you miss your way?
        A better seat you could not take
        Than on the margin of this lake.


Welcome!—I hail you to my glass:
    All welcome here you find;
Here let the cloud of trouble pass,
    Here be all care resigned.
        This fluid never fails to please,
        And drown the griefs of men or bees.


What forced you here we cannot know,
    And you will scarcely tell,
But cheery we would have you go
    And bid a glad farewell:
        On lighter wings we bid you fly—
        Your dart will now all foes defy.

Yet take not, oh! too deep a drink,
    And in this ocean die;
Here bigger bees than you might sink,
    Even bees full six feet high.
        Like Pharaoh, then, you would be said
        To perish in a sea of red.

Do as you please, your will is mine;
    Enjoy it without fear,
And your grave will be this glass of wine,
    Your epitaph—a tear;
        Go, take your seat in Charon's boat;
        We'll tell the hive, you died afloat.

## Stanzas

OCCASIONED BY THE RUINS OF A COUNTRY INN,
UNROOFED AND BLOWN DOWN IN A STORM

Where now these mingled ruins lie
A Temple once to Bacchus rose,
Beneath whose roof, aspiring high,
Full many a guest forgot his woes:

No more this dome, by tempests torn,
Affords a social safe retreat;
But ravens here, with eye forlorn,
And clustering bats henceforth shall meet.

The Priestess of this ruin'd shrine,
Unable to survive the stroke,
Presents no more the ruddy wine,
Her glasses gone, her china broke.

The friendly Host, whose social hand
Accosted strangers at the door,

Has left at length his wonted stand,
And greets the weary guest no more.

Old creeping time, that brings decay,
Might yet have spar'd these mouldering walls,
Alike beneath whose potent sway
A *temple* or a *tavern* falls.

Is this the place where mirth and joy,
Coy nymphs and sprightly lads were found?
Alas! no more the nymphs are coy,
No more the flowing bowls go round.

Is this the place where festive song
Deceiv'd the wintry hours away?
No more the swains the tune prolong,
No more the maidens join the lay:

Is this the place where Chloe slept
In downy beds of blue and green?
Dame Nature here no vigils kept,
No cold, unfeeling guards were seen.

'Tis gone!—and Chloe tempts no more,
Deep, unrelenting silence reigns;
Of all that pleas'd, that charm'd before,
The tottering chimney scarce remains!

Ye tyrant winds, whose ruffian blast
From locks and hinges rent the door.
And all the roof to ruin cast,
The roof that sheltered us before,

Your wrath appeased, I pray be kind
If Mopsus should the dome renew;
That we again may quaff his wine,
Again collect our jovial crew.

## Song of Thyrsis

The turtle on yon withered bough,
  That lately mourned her murdered mate,
Has found another comrade now—
  Such changes all await!
Again her drooping plume is drest,
Again she's willing to be blest
And takes her lover to her nest.

If nature has decreed it so
With all above, and all below,
Let us like them forget our woe,
  And not be killed with sorrow.
If I should quit your arms to-night
And chance to die before 't was light,
I would advise you—and you might—
  Love again to-morrow.

## On Observing a Large Red-streak Apple

In spite of ice, in spite of snow,
In spite of all the winds that blow,
In spite of hail and biting frost,
Suspended here I see you toss'd;
You still retain your wonted hold
Though days are short and nights are cold.

Amidst this system of decay
How could you have one wish to stay?
If fate or fancy kept you there
They meant you for a Solitaire.

Were it not better to descend,
Or in the cider mill to end
Than thus to shiver in the storm
And not a leaf to keep you warm—
A moment, then, had buried all,
Nor you have doomed so late a fall.

But should the stem to which you cling
Uphold you to another spring,
Another race would round you rise
And view the stranger with surprise,
And, peeping from the blossoms say
Away, old dotard, get away!

Alas! small pleasure can there be
To dwell, a hermit, on the tree—
Your old companions, all, are gone,
Have dropt, and perished, every one;
You only stay to face the blast,
A sad memento of the past.

Would fate or nature hear my prayer,
I would your bloom of youth repair
I would the wrongs of time restrain
And bring your blossom state again:
But fate and nature both say no;
And you, though late must perish too.

What can we say, what can we hope?
Ere from the branch I see you drop,
All I can do, all in my power
Will be to watch your parting hour:
When from the branch I see you fall,
A grave we dig a-south the wall.

There you shall sleep till from your core,
Of youngsters rises three or four;
These shall salute the coming spring
And red streaks to perfection bring
When years have brought them to their prime
And they shall have their summers time:
This, this is all you can attain,
And thus, I bid you, live again!

### On the Death of Benjamin Franklin

Thus, some tall tree that long hath stood
The glory of its native wood,
By storms destroyed, or length of years,
Demand the tribute of our tears.

The pile, that took long time to raise,
To dust returns by slow decays;
But, when its destined years are o'er,
We must regret the loss once more.

So long accustomed to your aid,
The world laments your exit made;
So long befriended by your art,
Philosopher, 't is hard to part!—

When monarchs tumble to the ground
Successors easily are found;
But, matchless Franklin! what a few
Can hope to rival such as you,
Who seized from kings their sceptered pride,
And turned the lightning's darts aside!

JOHN QUINCY ADAMS                              1767–1848

## To the Sun-Dial

UNDER THE WINDOW OF THE HALL OF THE HOUSE
OF REPRESENTATIVES OF THE UNITED STATES

Thou silent herald of Time's silent flight!
   Say, could'st thou speak, what warning voice were thine?
   Shade, who canst only show how others shine!
Dark, sullen witness of resplendent light
In day's broad glare, and when the moontide bright
   Of laughing fortune sheds the ray divine,
   Thy ready favors cheer us—but decline
The clouds of morning and the gloom of night.
Yet are thy counsels faithful, just, and wise;
   They bid us seize the moments as they pass—
Snatch the retrieveless sunbeam as it flies,
   Nor lose one sand of life's revolving glass—
Aspiring still, with energy sublime,
By virtuous deeds to give eternity to Time.

## JOSEPH HOPKINSON                    1770–1842

### Hail, Columbia

Hail, Columbia! happy land!
Hail, ye heroes! heaven-born band!
  Who fought and bled in Freedom's cause,
And when the storm of war was gone,
Enjoyed the peace your valor won.
    Let independence be our boast,
    Ever mindful what it cost;
    Ever grateful for the prize,
    Let its altar reach the skies.

    *Firm, united, let us be,*
    *Rallying round our Liberty;*
    *As a band of brothers joined,*
    *Peace and safety we shall find.*

Immortal patriots! rise once more:
Defend your rights, defend your shore:
  Let no rude foe, with impious hand,
Invade the shrine where sacred lies
Of toil and blood the well-earned prize.
    While offering peace sincere and just,
    In Heaven we place a manly trust,
    That truth and justice will prevail,
    And every scheme of bondage fail.

Sound, sound, the trump of Fame!
Let Washington's great name
  Ring through the world with loud applause;
Let every clime to Freedom dear,
Listen with a joyful ear.

With equal skill, and godlike power,
He governed in the fearful hour
Of horrid war; or guides, with ease,
The happier times of honest peace.

Behold the chief who now commands,
Once more to serve his country, stands—
    The rock on which the storm will beat;
But, armed in virtue firm and true,
His hopes are fixed on heaven and you.
    When hope was sinking in dismay,
    And glooms obscured Columbia's day,
    His steady mind, from changes free,
    Resolved on death or liberty.

*Firm, united, let us be,*
*Rallying round our Liberty;*
*As a band of brothers joined,*
*Peace and safety we shall find.*

# FRANCIS SCOTT KEY                    1779–1843

## The Star-Spangled Banner

Oh, say, can you see, by the dawn's early light,
    What so proudly we hailed at the twilight's last gleaming,
Whose broad stripes and bright stars through the perilous
        fight,
    O'er the ramparts we watched were so gallantly streaming?
And the rockets' red glare, the bombs bursting in air,
Gave proof through the night that our flag was still there.
Oh, say, does that star-spangled banner yet wave
O'er the land of the free, and the home of the brave?

On the shore, dimly seen through the mists of the deep,
  Where the foe's haughty host in dread silence reposes,
What is that which the breeze, o'er the towering steep,
  As it fitfully blows, half conceals, half discloses?
Now it catches the gleam of the morning's first beam,
In full glory reflected, now shines on the stream.
'Tis the star-spangled banner; oh, long may it wave
O'er the land of the free, and the home of the brave!

And where is that band who so vauntingly swore
  That the havoc of war and the battle's confusion
A home and a country should leave us no more?
  Their blood has washed out their foul footsteps' pollution.
No refuge could save the hireling and slave
From the terror of flight, or the gloom of the grave:
And the star-spangled banner in triumph doth wave
O'er the land of the free, and the home of the brave!

Oh! thus be it ever when freemen shall stand
  Between their loved homes and the war's desolation!
Blest with victory and peace, may the heaven-rescued land
  Praise the Power that hath made and preserved us a nation!
Then conquer we must, for our cause it is just,
And this be our motto: "In God is our trust!"
And the star-spangled banner in triumph shall wave,
O'er the land of the free, and the home of the brave!

JOHN PIERPONT                    1785–1866

## The Pilgrim Fathers

The Pilgrim Fathers,—where are they?
   The waves that brought them o'er
Still roll in the bay, and throw their spray
   As they break along the shore;
Still roll in the bay, as they rolled that day
   When the Mayflower moored below;
When the sea around was black with storms,
   And white the shore with snow.

The mists that wrapped the Pilgrim's sleep
   Still brood upon the tide;
And his rocks yet keep their watch by the deep
   To stay its waves of pride.
But the snow-white sail that he gave to the gale,
   When the heavens looked dark, is gone,—
As an angel's wing through an opening cloud
   Is seen, and then withdrawn.

The pilgrim exile,—sainted name!
   The hill whose icy brow
Rejoiced, when he came, in the morning's flame,
   In the morning's flame burns now.
And the moon's cold light, as it lay that night
   On the hillside and the sea,
Still lies where he laid his houseless head,—
   But the Pilgrim! where is he?

The Pilgrim Fathers are at rest:
   When summer's throned on high,
And the world's warm breast is in verdure drest,
   Go, stand on the hill where they lie.

The earliest ray of the golden day
  On that hallowed spot is cast;
And the evening sun, as he leaves the world,
  Looks kindly on that spot last.

The Pilgrim spirit has not fled:
  It walks in noon's broad light;
And it watches the bed of the glorious dead,
  With the holy stars by night.
It watches the bed of the brave who have bled,
  And still guard this ice-bound shore,
Till the waves of the bay, where the Mayflower lay,
  Shall foam and freeze no more.

## Whittling

The Yankee boy, before he's sent to school,
Well knows the mysteries of that magic tool,
The pocket-knife. To that his wistful eye
Turns, while he hears his mother's lullaby;
His hoarded cents he gladly gives to get it,
Then leaves no stone unturned till he can whet it;
And in the education of the lad
No little part that implement hath had.
His pocket-knife to the young whittler brings
A growing knowledge of material things.

Projectiles, music, and the sculptor's art,
His chestnut whistle and his shingle dart,
His elder popgun with its hickory rod,
Its sharp explosion and rebounding wad,
His cornstalk fiddle, and the deeper tone
That murmurs from his pumpkin-stalk trombone,
Conspire to teach the boy. To these succeed
His bow, his arrow of a feathered seed,

His windmill, raised the passing breeze to win,
His water-wheel, that turns upon a pin;
Or, if his father lives upon the shore,
You'll see his ship, "beam ends upon the floor,"
Full rigged with raking masts, and timbers stanch,
And waiting near the wash-tub for a launch.

Thus by his genius and his jack-knife driven,
Erelong he'll solve you any problem given;
Make any gimcrack musical or mute,
A plough, a couch, an organ or a flute;
Make you a locomotive or a clock,
Cut a canal, or build a floating-dock,
Or lead forth Beauty from a marble block;—
Make anything in short, for sea or shore,
From a child's rattle to a seventy-four;—
Make it, said I?—Ay, when he undertakes it,
He'll make the thing and the machine that makes it.

And when the thing is made,—whether it be
To move on earth, in air, or on the sea;
Whether on water, o'er the waves to glide,
Or upon land to roll, revolve, or slide;
Whether to whirl or jar, to strike or ring,
Whether it be a piston or a spring,
Wheel, pulley, tube sonorous, wood or brass,
The thing designed shall surely come to pass;
For, when his hand's upon it, you may know
That there's go in it, and he'll make it go.

## Warren's Address at Bunker Hill

Stand! the ground's your own, my braves!
Will ye give it up to slaves?
Will ye look for greener graves?
    Hope ye mercy still?
What's the mercy despots feel?
Hear it in that battle-peal!
Read it in yon bristling steel!
    Ask it—ye who will.

Fear ye foes who kill for hire?
Will ye to your homes retire?
Look behind you—they're afire!
    And, before you, see
Who have done it! From the vale
On they come—and will ye quail?
Leaden rain and iron hail
    Let their welcome be!

In the God of battles trust.
Die we may, and die we must.
But, O, where can dust to dust
    Be consigned so well
As where heaven its dews shall shed
On the martyred patriot's bed,
And the rocks shall raise their head
    Of his deeds to tell.

SAMUEL WOODWORTH                    1785–1842

### The Bucket

How dear to this heart are the scenes of my childhood,
    When fond recollection presents them to view!
The orchard, the meadow, the deep-tangled wild-wood,
    And every loved spot which my infancy knew!
The wide-spreading pond, and the mill that stood by it,
    The bridge, and the rock where the cataract fell,
The cot of my father, the dairy-house nigh it,
    And e'en the rude bucket that hung in the well—
The old oaken bucket, the iron-bound bucket,
The moss-covered bucket which hung in the well.

That moss-covered vessel I hailed as a treasure,
    For often at noon, when returned from the field,
I found it the source of an exquisite pleasure,
    The purest and sweetest that nature can yield.
How ardent I seized it, with hands that were glowing,
    And quick to the white-pebbled bottom it fell;
Then soon, with the emblem of truth overflowing,
    And dripping with coolness, it rose from the well—
The old oaken bucket, the iron-bound bucket,
The moss-covered bucket arose from the well.

How sweet from the green mossy brim to receive it,
    As poised on the curb it inclined to my lips!
Not a full blushing goblet could tempt me to leave it,
    The brightest that beauty or revelry sips.
And now, far removed from the loved habitation,
    The tear of regret will intrusively swell,
As fancy reverts to my father's plantation,
    And sighs for the bucket that hangs in the well—
The old oaken bucket, the iron-bound bucket,
The moss-covered bucket that hangs in the well!

# EMMA HART WILLARD                          1787–1870

### *Rocked in the Cradle of the Deep*

Rocked in the cradle of the deep
I lay me down in peace to sleep;
Secure I rest upon the wave,
For thou, O Lord! hast power to save.
I know thou wilt not slight my call,
For thou dost mark the sparrow's fall;
And calm and peaceful shall I sleep,
Rocked in the cradle of the deep.

When in the dead of night I lie
And gaze upon the trackless sky,
The star-bespangled heavenly scroll,
The boundless waters as they roll,—
I feel thy wondrous power to save
From perils of the stormy wave:
Rocked in the cradle of the deep,
I calmly rest and soundly sleep.

And such the trust that still were mine,
Though stormy winds swept o'er the brine,
Or though the tempest's fiery breath
Roused me from sleep to wreck and death.
In ocean cave, still safe with thee
The germ of immortality!
And calm and peaceful shall I sleep,
Rocked in the cradle of the deep.

RICHARD HENRY DANA                    1787–1879

*The Little Beach Bird*

Thou little bird, thou dweller by the sea,
  Why takest thou its melancholy voice?
      Why with that boding cry
      O'er the waves dost thou fly?
O, rather, bird, with me
  Through the fair land rejoice!

Thy flitting form comes ghostly dim and pale,
  As driven by a beating storm at sea;
      Thy cry is weak and scared,
      As if thy mates had shared
The doom of us. Thy wail—
  What does it bring to me?

Thou call'st along the sand, and haunt'st the surge,
  Restless and sad; as if, in strange accord
      With motion and with roar
      Of waves that drive to shore,
One spirit did ye urge—
  The Mystery—the Word.

Of thousands thou both sepulchre and pall,
  Old ocean, art! A requiem o'er the dead,
      From out thy gloomy cells,
      A tale of mourning tells,—
Tells of man's woe and fall,
  His sinless glory fled.

Then turn thee, little bird, and take thy flight
  Where the complaining sea shall sadness bring
      Thy spirit nevermore.
      Come, quit with me the shore,
For gladness and the light,
  Where birds of summer sing.

RICHARD HENRY WILDE                         1789–1847

### My Life Is Like the Summer Rose

My life is like the summer rose,
   That opens to the morning sky,
But, ere the shades of evening close,
   Is scattered on the ground—to die!
Yet on the rose's humble bed
The sweetest dews of night are shed,
As if she wept the waste to see—
But none shall weep a tear for me!

My life is like the autumn leaf
   That trembles in the moon's pale ray:
Its hold is frail—its date is brief,
   Restless—and soon to pass away!
Yet, ere that leaf shall fall and fade,
The parent tree will mourn its shade,
The winds bewail the leafless tree—
But none shall breathe a sigh for me!

My life is like the prints, which feet
   Have left on Tampa's desert strand;
Soon as the rising tide shall beat,
   All trace will vanish from the sand;
Yet, as if grieving to efface
All vestige of the human race,
On that lone shore loud moans the sea—
But none, alas! shall mourn for me!

FITZ-GREENE HALLECK          1790–1867

### On the Death of Joseph Rodman Drake[1]

Green be the turf above thee,
    Friend of my better days!
None knew thee but to love thee,
    Nor named thee but to praise.

Tears fell when thou wert dying,
    From eyes unused to weep,
And long, where thou art lying,
    Will tears the cold turf steep.

When hearts, whose truth was proven,
    Like thine, are laid in earth,
There should a wreath be woven
    To tell the world their worth;

And I who woke each morrow
    To clasp thy hand in mine,
Who shared thy joy and sorrow,
    Whose weal and woe were thine;

It should be mine to braid it
    Around thy faded brow,
But I've in vain essayed it,
    And feel I cannot now.

While memory bids me weep thee,
    Nor thoughts nor words are free,—
The grief is fixed too deeply
    That mourns a man like thee.

[1] See pages 32, 33.

LYDIA SIGOURNEY                            1791–1865

### Indian Names

Ye say they all have pass'd away,
    That noble race and brave,
That their light canoes have vanish'd
    From off the crested wave.
That 'mid the forests where they roam'd
    There rings no hunter's shout;
But their name is on your waters,
    Ye may not wash it out.

'Tis where Ontario's billow
    Like Ocean's surge is curl'd;
Where strong Niagara's thunders wake
    The echo of the world;
Where red Missouri bringeth
    Rich tributes from the west,
And Rappahannock sweetly sleeps
    On green Virginia's breast.

Ye say, their cone-like cabins,
    That cluster'd o'er the vale,
Have fled away like wither'd leaves
    Before the autumn gale:
But their memory liveth on your hills,
    Their baptism on your shore;
Your everlasting rivers speak
    Their dialect of yore.

Old Massachusetts wears it
    Within her lordly crown,
And broad Ohio bears it
    'Mid all her young renown;

Connecticut hath wreathed it
  Where her quiet foliage waves,
And bold Kentucky breathed it hoarse
  Through all her ancient caves.

Wachuset hides its lingering voice
  Within his rocky heart,
And Alleghany graves its tone
  Throughout his lofty chart:
Monadnock on his forehead hoar
  Doth seal the sacred trust;
Your mountains build their monument,
  Though ye destroy their dust.

# CHARLES SPRAGUE                    1791–1875

## The Winged Worshippers

ADDRESSED TO TWO SWALLOWS THAT FLEW INTO THE
CHAUNCY PLACE CHURCH DURING DIVINE SERVICE

Gay, guiltless pair,
What seek ye from the fields of heaven?
  Ye have no need of prayer;
Ye have no sins to be forgiven.

Why perch ye here,
Where mortals to their Maker bend?
  Can your pure spirits fear
The God ye never could offend?

Ye never knew
The crimes for which we come to weep.
  Penance is not for you,
Blessed wanderers of the *upper deep*.

To you 't is given
To wake sweet Nature's untaught lays;
   Beneath the arch of heaven
To chirp away a life of praise.

Then spread each wing
Far, far above, o'er lakes and lands,
   And join the choirs that sing
In yon blue dome not reared with hands.

Or, if ye stay,
To note the consecrated hour,
   Teach me the airy way,
And let me try your envied power.

Above the crowd
On upward wings could I but fly,
   I'd bathe in yon bright cloud,
And seek the stars that gem the sky.

'T were heaven indeed
Through fields of trackless light to soar,
   On Nature's charms to feed,
And Nature's own great God adore.

JOSEPH RODMAN DRAKE                    1795–1820

### The American Flag

I

When Freedom from her mountain height
　Unfurl'd her standard to the air,
She tore the azure robe of night,
　And set the stars of glory there.
She mingled with its gorgeous dyes
The milky baldric of the skies,
And striped its pure celestial white
With streakings of the morning light;
Then from his mansion in the sun
She call'd her eagle bearer down,
And gave into his mighty hand
The symbol of her chosen land.

II

Majestic monarch of the cloud,
　Who rear'st aloft thy regal form,
To hear the tempest trumpings loud
And see the lightning lances driven,
　When strive the warriors of the storm,
And rolls the thunder-drum of heaven,
Child of the sun! to thee 'tis given
　To guard the banner of the free,
To hover in the sulphur smoke,
To ward away the battle stroke,
And bid its blendings shine afar,
Like rainbows on the cloud of war,
　The harbingers of victory!

III

Flag of the brave! thy folds shall fly,
　The sign of hope and triumph high,
When speaks the signal trumpet tone,
　And the long line comes gleaming on.

Ere yet the life-blood, warm and wet,
   Has dimm'd the glistening bayonet,
Each soldier eye shall brightly turn
   To where thy sky-born glories burn;
And, as his springing steps advance,
Catch war and vengeance from the glance.
And when the cannon-mouthings loud
   Heave in wild wreaths the battle-shroud
And gory sabres rise and fall
Like shoots of flame on midnight's pall;
   Then shall thy meteor glances glow,
And cowering foes shall shrink beneath
   Each gallant arm that strikes below
That lovely messenger of death.

IV

Flag of the seas! on ocean wave
Thy stars shall glitter o'er the brave;
When death, careering on the gale,
Sweeps darkly round the bellied sail,
And freighted waves rush wildly back
Before the broadside's reeling rack,
Each dying wanderer of the sea
Shall look at once to heaven and thee,
And smile to see thy splendour fly
In triumph o'er his closing eye.

V

Flag of the free heart's hope and home!
   By angel hands to valor given;
The stars have lit the welkin dome,
   And all thy hues were born in heaven.
Forever float that standard sheet!
   Where breathes the foe but falls before us,
With Freedom's soil beneath our feet,
   And Freedom's banner streaming o'er us!

JAMES GATES PERCIVAL                    1795–1856

### To Seneca Lake

On thy fair bosom, silver lake,
  The wild swan spreads his snowy sail,
And round his breast the ripples break,
  As down he bears before the gale.

On thy fair bosom, waveless stream,
  The dipping paddle echoes far,
And flashes in the moonlight gleam,
  And bright reflects the polar star.

The waves along thy pebbly shore,
  As blows the north-wind, heave their foam,
And curl around the dashing oar,
  As late the boatman hies him home.

How sweet, at set of sun, to view
  Thy golden mirror spreading wide,
And see the mist of mantling blue
  Float round the distant mountain's side.

At midnight hour, as shines the moon,
  A sheet of silver spreads below,
And swift she cuts, at highest noon,
  Light clouds, like wreaths of purest snow.

On thy fair bosom, silver lake,
  O, I could ever sweep the oar,
When early birds at morning wake,
  And evening tells us toil is o'er!

## The Coral Grove

Deep in the wave is a coral grove,
Where the purple mullet and gold-fish rove;
Where the sea-flower spreads its leaves of blue
That never are wet with falling dew,
But in bright and changeful beauty shine
Far down in the green and glassy brine.
The floor is of sand, like the mountain drift,
And the pearl-shells spangle the flinty snow;
From coral rocks the sea-plants lift
Their boughs, where the tides and billows flow:
The water is calm and still below,
For the winds and waves are absent there,
And the sands are bright as the stars that glow
In the motionless fields of upper air.
There, with its waving blade of green,
The sea-flag streams through the silent water,
And the crimson leaf of the dulse is seen
To blush, like a banner bathed in slaughter.
There, with a light and easy motion,
The fan-coral sweeps through the clear deep sea;
And the yellow and scarlet tufts of ocean
Are bending like corn on the upland lea:
And life, in rare and beautiful forms,
Is sporting amid those bowers of stone,
And is safe when the wrathful Spirit of storms
Has made the top of the wave his own.
And when the ship from his fury flies,
Where the myriad voices of Ocean roar;
When the wind-god frowns in the murky skies,
And demons are waiting the wreck on shore;
Then, far below, in the peaceful sea,
The purple mullet and gold-fish rove,
Where the waters murmur tranquilly,
Through the bending twigs of the coral grove.

## WILLIAM CULLEN BRYANT                1794–1878

### America

O mother of a mighty race,
Yet lovely in thy youthful grace!
The elder dames, thy haughty peers,
Admire and hate thy blooming years;
      With words of shame
And taunts of scorn they join thy name.

For on thy cheeks the glow is spread
That tints thy morning hills with red;
Thy step,—the wild deer's rustling feet
Within thy woods are not more fleet;
      Thy hopeful eye
Is bright as thine own sunny sky.

Ay, let them rail, those haughty ones,
While safe thou dwellest with thy sons.
They do not know how loved thou art,
How many a fond and fearless heart
      Would rise to throw
Its life between thee and the foe.

They know not, in their hate and pride,
What virtues with thy children bide,—
How true, how good, thy graceful maids
Make bright, like flowers, the valley shades;
      What generous men
Spring, like thine oaks, by hill and glen;

What cordial welcomes greet the guest
By thy lone rivers of the west;

How faith is kept, and truth revered,
And man is loved, and God is feared,
 In woodland homes,
And where the ocean border foams.


There's freedom at thy gates, and rest
For earth's down-trodden and opprest,
A shelter for the hunted head,
For the starved laborer toil and bread.
 Power, at thy bounds,
Stops, and calls back his baffled hounds.


O fair young mother! on thy brow
Shall sit a nobler grace than now.
Deep in the brightness of thy skies,
The thronging years in glory rise,
 And, as they fleet,
Drop strength and riches at thy feet.


Thine eye, with every coming hour,
Shall brighten, and thy form shall tower;
And when thy sisters, elder born,
Would brand thy name with words of scorn,
 Before thine eye
Upon their lips the taunt shall die.


### To the Fringed Gentian


Thou blossom, bright with autumn dew,
And colored with the heaven's own blue,
That openest when the quiet light
Succeeds the keen and frosty night;


Thou comest not when violets lean
O'er wandering brooks and springs unseen,

Or columbines, in purple dressed,
Nod o'er the ground-bird's hidden nest.

Thou waitest late, and com'st alone,
When woods are bare and birds are flown,
And frosts and shortening days portend
The aged Year is near his end.

Then doth thy sweet and quiet eye
Look through its fringes to the sky,
Blue—blue—as if that sky let fall
A flower from its cerulean wall.

I would that thus, when I shall see
The hour of death draw near to me,
Hope, blossoming within my heart,
May look to heaven as I depart.

## O, Fairest of the Rural Maids!

O, fairest of the rural maids!
Thy birth was in the forest shades;
Green boughs, and glimpses of the sky,
Were all that met thine infant eye.

Thy sports, thy wanderings, when a child,
Were ever in the sylvan wild,
And all the beauty of the place
Is in thy heart and on thy face.

The twilight of the trees and rocks
Is in the light shade of thy locks;
Thy step is as the wind, that weaves
Its playful way among the leaves.

Thine eyes are springs, in whose serene
And silent waters heaven is seen;
Their lashes are the herbs that look
On their young figures in the brook.

The forest depths, by foot unpressed,
Are not more sinless than thy breast;
The holy peace, that fills the air
Of those calm solitudes, is there.

## The Yellow Violet

When beechen buds begin to swell,
   And woods the blue-bird's warble know,
The yellow violet's modest bell
   Peeps from the last year's leaves below.

Ere russet fields their green resume,
   Sweet flower, I love, in forest bare,
To meet thee, when thy faint perfume
   Alone is in the virgin air.

Of all her train, the hands of Spring
   First plant thee in the watery mould,
And I have seen thee blossoming
   Beside the snow-bank's edges cold.

Thy parent sun, who bade thee view
   Pale skies, and chilling moisture sip,
Has bathed thee in his own bright hue,
   And streaked with jet thy glowing lip.

Yet slight thy form, and low thy seat,
   And earthward bent thy gentle eye,

Unapt the passing view to meet,
  When loftier flowers are flaunting nigh.

Oft, in the sunless April day,
  Thy early smile has stayed my walk;
But midst the gorgeous blooms of May,
  I passed thee on thy humble stalk.

So they, who climb to wealth, forget
  The friends in darker fortunes tried.
I copied them—but I regret
  That I should ape the ways of pride.

And when again the genial hour
  Awakes the painted tribes of light,
I'll not o'erlook the modest flower
  That made the woods of April bright.

### Inscription for the Entrance to a Wood

Stranger, if thou hast learned a truth which needs
No school of long experience, that the world
Is full of guilt and misery, and hast seen
Enough of all its sorrows, crimes, and cares,
To tire thee of it, enter this wild wood
And view the haunts of Nature. The calm shade
Shall bring a kindred calm, and the sweet breeze
That makes the green leaves dance, shall waft a balm
To thy sick heart. Thou wilt find nothing here
Of all that pained thee in the haunts of men,
And made thee loathe thy life. The primal curse
Fell, it is true, upon the unsinning earth,
But not in vengeance. God hath yoked to Guilt
Her pale tormentor, Misery. Hence these shades
Are still the abodes of gladness; the thick roof

Of green and stirring branches is alive
And musical with birds, that sing and sport
In wantonness of spirit; while below
The squirrel, with raised paws and form erect,
Chirps merrily. Throngs of insects in the shade
Try their thin wings and dance in the warm beam
That waked them into life. Even the green trees
Partake the deep contentment; as they bend
To the soft winds, the sun from the blue sky
Looks in and sheds a blessing on the scene.
Scarce less the cleft-born wild-flower seems to enjoy
Existence, than the winged plunderer
That sucks its sweets. The mossy rocks themselves,
And the old and ponderous trunks of prostrate trees
That lead from knoll to knoll a causey rude,
Or bridge the sunken brook, and their dark roots,
With all their earth upon them, twisting high,
Breathe fixed tranquillity. The rivulet
Sends forth glad sounds, and tripping o'er its bed
Of pebbly sands, or leaping down the rocks,
Seems, with continuous laughter, to rejoice
In its own being. Softly tread the marge,
Lest from her midway perch thou scare the wren
That dips her bill in water. The cool wind,
That stirs the stream in play, shall come to thee,
Like one that loves thee nor will let thee pass
Ungreeted, and shall give its light embrace.

### June

I gazed upon the glorious sky,
    And the green mountains round,
And thought that when I came to lie
    At rest within the ground,

'T were pleasant that in flowery June,
When brooks send up a cheerful tune,
   And groves a cheerful sound,
The sexton's hand, my grave to make,
The rich, green mountain turf should break.

A cell within the frozen mould,
   A coffin borne through sleet,
And icy clods above it rolled,
   While fierce the tempests beat—
Away! I will not think of these—
Blue be the sky and soft the breeze,
   Earth green beneath the feet,
And be the damp mould gently pressed
Into my narrow place of rest.

There, through the long, long, summer hours
   The golden light should lie,
And thick young herbs and groups of flowers
   Stand in their beauty by.
The oriole should build and tell
His love-tale close beside my cell;
   The idle butterfly
Should rest him there, and there be heard
The housewife bee and humming-bird.

And what if cheerful shouts at noon
   Come, from the village sent,
Or song of maids beneath the moon
   With fairy laughter blent?
And what if, in the evening light,
Betrothed lovers walk in sight
   Of my low monument?
I would the lovely scene around
Might know no sadder sight nor sound.

I know that I no more should see
    The season's glorious show,
Nor would its brightness shine for me,
    Nor its wild music flow;
But if, around my place of sleep,
The friends I love should come to weep,
    They might not haste to go.
Soft airs, and song, and light and bloom
Should keep them lingering by my tomb.

These to their softened hearts should bear
    The thought of what has been,
And speak of one who cannot share
    The gladness of the scene;
Whose part, in all the pomp that fills
The circuit of the summer hills,
    Is that his grave is green;
And deeply would their hearts rejoice
To hear again his living voice.

## Thanatopsis

To him who in the love of Nature holds
Communion with her visible forms, she speaks
A various language; for his gayer hours
She has a voice of gladness, and a smile
And eloquence of beauty, and she glides
Into his darker musings, with a mild
And healing sympathy, that steals away
Their sharpness ere he is aware. When thoughts
Of the last bitter hour come like a blight
Over thy spirit, and sad images
Of the stern agony, and shroud, and pall,
And breathless darkness, and the narrow house,
Make thee to shudder, and grow sick at heart;—

Go forth, under the open sky, and list
To Nature's teachings, while from all around—
Earth and her waters, and the depths of air,—
Comes a still voice—Yet a few days, and thee
The all-beholding sun shall see no more
In all his course; nor yet in the cold ground,
Where thy pale form was laid, with many tears,
Nor in the embrace of ocean, shall exist
Thy image. Earth, that nourished thee, shall claim
Thy growth, to be resolved to earth again,
And, lost each human trace, surrendering up
Thine individual being, shalt thou go
To mix for ever with the elements,
To be a brother to the insensible rock
And to the sluggish clod, which the rude swain
Turns with his share, and treads upon. The oak
Shall send his roots abroad, and pierce thy mould.

Yet not to thine eternal resting-place
Shalt thou retire alone,—nor couldst thou wish
Couch more magnificent. Thou shalt lie down
With patriarchs of the infant world—with kings,
The powerful of the earth—the wise, the good,
Fair forms, and hoary seers of ages past,
All in one mighty sepulchre. The hills
Rock-ribbed and ancient as the sun; the vales
Stretching in pensive quietness between;
The venerable woods; rivers that move
In majesty, and the complaining brooks
That make the meadows green; and, poured round all,
Old ocean's grey and melancholy waste—
Are but the solemn decorations all
Of the great tomb of man. The golden sun,
The planets, all the infinite host of heaven,
Are shining on the sad abodes of death,

Through the still lapse of ages. All that tread
The globe are but a handful to the tribes
That slumber in its bosom.—Take the wings
Of morning, traverse Barca's desert sands,
Or lose thyself in the continuous woods
Where rolls the Oregon, and hears no sound,
Save his own dashings—yet—the dead are there:
And millions in those solitudes, since first
The flight of years began, have laid them down
In their last sleep—the dead reign there alone.
So shalt thou rest, and what if thou withdraw
In silence from the living, and no friend
Take note of thy departure? All that breathe
Will share thy destiny. The gay will laugh
When thou art gone, the solemn brood of care
Plod on, and each one as before will chase
His favourite phantom; yet all these shall leave
Their mirth and their employments, and shall come,
And make their bed with thee. As the long train
Of ages glide away, the sons of men,
The youth in life's green spring, and he who goes
In the full strength of years, matron, and maid,
And the sweet babe, and the grey-headed man—
Shall one by one be gathered to thy side,
By those, who in their turn shall follow them.

So live, that when thy summons comes to join
The innumerable caravan, which moves
To that mysterious realm, where each shall take
His chamber in the silent halls of death,
Thou go not, like the quarry-slave at night,
Scourged to his dungeon, but, sustained and soothed
By an unfaltering trust, approach thy grave
Like one who wraps the drapery of his couch
About him, and lies down to pleasant dreams.

### To a Waterfowl

Whither, midst falling dew,
While glow the heavens with the last steps of day,
Far, through their rosy depths, dost thou pursue
    Thy solitary way?

Vainly the fowler's eye
Might mark thy distant flight to do thee wrong,
As, darkly seen against the crimson sky,
    Thy figure floats along.

Seek'st thou the plashy brink
Of weedy lake, or marge of river wide,
Or where the rocking billows rise and sink
    On the chafed ocean-side?

There is a Power whose care
Teaches thy way along that pathless coast—
The desert and illimitable air—
    Lone wandering, but not lost.

All day thy wings have fanned,
At that far height, the cold, thin atmosphere,
Yet stoop not, weary, to the welcome land,
    Though the dark night is near.

And soon that toil shall end;
Soon shalt thou find a summer home, and rest,
And scream among thy fellows; reeds shall bend,
    Soon, o'er thy sheltered nest.

Thou'rt gone, the abyss of heaven
Hath swallowed up thy form; yet, on my heart

Deeply has sunk the lesson thou hast given,
   And shall not soon depart.

He who, from zone to zone,
Guides through the boundless sky thy certain flight,
In the long way that I must tread alone,
   Will lead my steps aright.

### The Death of Lincoln

Oh, slow to smite and swift to spare,
   Gentle and merciful and just!
Who, in the fear of God, didst bear
   The sword of power, a nation's trust!

In sorrow by thy bier we stand,
   Amid the awe that hushes all,
And speak the anguish of a land
   That shook with horror at thy fall.

Thy task is done; the bond are free:
   We bear thee to an honored grave,
Whose proudest monument shall be
   The broken fetters of the slave.

Pure was thy life; its bloody close
   Hath placed thee with the sons of light,
Among the noble host of those
   Who perished in the cause of Right.

EDWARD COOTE PINKNEY       1802–1828

### A Health

I fill this cup to one made up
   Of loveliness alone,
A woman, of her gentle sex
   The seeming paragon;
To whom the better elements
   And kindly stars have given
A form so fair, that, like the air,
   'T is less of earth than heaven.

Her every tone is music's own,
   Like those of morning birds,
And something more than melody
   Dwells ever in her words;
The coinage of her heart are they,
   And from her lips each flows,
As one may see the burdened bee
   Forth issue from the rose.

Affections are as thoughts to her,
   The measures of her hours;
Her feelings have the fragrancy,
   The freshness of young flowers;
And lovely passions, changing oft,
   So fill her, she appears
The image of themselves by turns,—
   The idol of past years!

Of her bright face one glance will trace
   A picture on the brain,
And of her voice in echoing hearts
   A sound must long remain;

But memory, such as mine of her,
 So very much endears,
When death is nigh my latest sigh
 Will not be life's, but hers.


I fill this cup to one made up
 Of loveliness alone,
A woman, of her gentle sex
 The seeming paragon.
Her health! and would on earth there stood
 Some more of such a frame,
That life might be all poetry,
 And weariness a name.


## A Serenade

Look out upon the stars, my love,
 And shame them with thine eyes,
On which, than on the lights above,
 There hang more destinies.
Night's beauty is the harmony
 Of blending shades and light;
Then, lady, up,—look out, and be
 A sister to the night!


Sleep not! thine image wakes for aye
 Within my watching breast:
Sleep not! from her soft sleep should fly
 Who robs all hearts of rest.
Nay, lady, from thy slumbers break,
 And make this darkness gay
With looks, whose brightness well might make
 Of darker nights a day.

## Votive Song

I burn no incense, hang no wreath
  On this thine early tomb:
Such cannot cheer the place of death,
  But only mock its gloom.
Here odorous smoke and breathing flower
  No grateful influence shed;
They lose their perfume and their power,
  When offered to the dead.

And if, as is the Afghan's creed,
  The spirit may return,
A disembodied sense to feed,
  On fragrance, near its urn,—
It is enough that she, whom thou
  Didst love in living years,
Sits desolate beside it now,
  And fall these heavy tears.

## RALPH WALDO EMERSON                    1803–1882

### *The Rhodora*

ON BEING ASKED, WHENCE IS THE FLOWER?

In May, when sea-winds pierced our solitudes,
I found the fresh Rhodora in the woods,
Spreading its leafless blooms in a damp nook,
To please the desert and the sluggish brook.
The purple petals, fallen in the pool,
Made the black water with their beauty gay;
Here might the red-bird come his plumes to cool,
And court the flower that cheapens his array.
Rhodora! if the sages ask thee why
This charm is wasted on the earth and sky,
Tell them, dear, that if eyes were made for seeing,
Then Beauty is its own excuse for being:
Why thou wert there, O rival of the rose!
I never thought to ask, I never knew;
But, in my simple ignorance, suppose
The self-same Power that brought me there brought you.

### *Forbearance*

Hast thou named all the birds without a gun?
Loved the wood-rose, and left it on its stalk?
At rich men's tables eaten bread and pulse?
Unarmed, faced danger with a heart of trust?
And loved so well a high behaviour,
In man or maid, that thou from speech refrained,
Nobility more nobly to repay?
O, be my friend, and teach me to be thine!

## The Snow-Storm

Announced by all the trumpets of the sky,
Arrives the snow, and, driving o'er the fields,
Seems nowhere to alight: the whited air
Hides hills and woods, the river, and the heaven,
And veils the farm-house at the garden's end.
The sled and traveller stopped, the courier's feet
Delayed, all friends shut out, the housemates sit
Around the radiant fireplace, enclosed
In a tumultuous privacy of storm.

Come see the north wind's masonry.
Out of an unseen quarry evermore
Furnished with tile, the fierce artificer
Curves his white bastions with projected roof
Round every windward stake, or tree, or door.
Speeding, the myriad-handed, his wild work
So fanciful, so savage, nought cares he
For number or proportion. Mockingly,
On coop or kennel he hangs Parian wreaths;
A swan-like form invests the hidden thorn;
Fills up the farmer's lane from wall to wall,
Maugre the farmer's sighs; and, at the gate,
A tapering turret overtops the work.
And when his hours are numbered, and the world
Is all his own, retiring, as he were not,
Leaves, when the sun appears, astonished Art
To mimic in slow structures, stone by stone,
Built in an age, the mad wind's night-work,
The frolic architecture of the snow.

## Wealth

Who shall tell what did befall,
Far away in time, when once,
Over the lifeless ball,
Hung idle stars and suns?
What god the element obeyed?
Wings of what wind the lichen bore,
Wafting the puny seeds of power,
Which, lodged in rock, the rock abrade?
And well the primal pioneer
Knew the strong task to it assigned,
Patient through Heaven's enormous year
To build in matter home for mind.
From air the creeping centuries drew
The matted thicket low and wide,
This must the leaves of ages strew
The granite slab to clothe and hide,
Ere wheat can wave its golden pride.
What smiths, and in what furnace, rolled
(In dizzy aeons dim and mute
The reeling brain can ill compute)
Copper and iron, lead and gold?
What oldest star the fame can save
Of races perishing to pave
The planet with a floor of lime?
Dust is their pyramid and mole:
Who saw what ferns and palms were pressed
Under the tumbling mountain's breast,
In the safe herbal of the coal?
But when the quarried means were piled,
All is waste and worthless, till
Arrives the wise selecting will,
And, out of slime and chaos, Wit
Draws the threads of fair and fit.

Then temples rose, and towns, and marts,
The shop of toil, the hall of arts;
Then flew the sail across the seas
To feed the North from tropic trees;
The storm-wind wove, the torrent span,
Where they were bid the rivers ran;
New slaves fulfilled the poet's dream,
Galvanic wire, strong-shouldered steam.
Then docks were built, and crops were stored,
And ingots added to the hoard.
But, though light-headed man forget,
Remembering Matter pays her debt:
Still, though her motes and masses, draw
Electric thrills and ties of Law,
Which bind the strength of Nature wild
To the conscience of a child.

## Fate

Deep in the man sits fast his fate
To mould his fortunes mean or great:
Unknown to Cromwell as to me
Was Cromwell's measure or degree;
Unknown to him, as to his horse,
If he than his groom be better or worse.
He works, plots, fights, in rude affairs,
With squires, lords, kings, his craft compares,
Till late he learned, through doubt and fear,
Broad England harboured not his peer:
Obeying Time, the last to own
The Genius from its cloudy throne.
For the prevision is allied
Unto the thing so signified;
Or say, the foresight that awaits
Is the same Genius that creates.

## *Forerunners*

Long I followed happy guides,
I could never reach their sides;
Their step is forth, and, ere the day,
Breaks up their leaguer, and away.
Keen my sense, my heart was young,
Right good-will my sinews strung,
But no speed of mine avails
To hunt upon their shining trails.
On and away, their hasting feet
Make the morning proud and sweet;
Flowers they strew—I catch the scent;
Or tone of silver instrument
Leaves on the wind melodious trace;
Yet I could never see their face.
On eastern hills I see their smokes,
Mixed with mist by distant lochs.
I met many travellers
Who the road had surely kept;
They saw not my fine revellers,—
These had crossed them while they slept.
Some had heard their fair report,
In the country or the court.
Fleetest couriers alive
Never yet could once arrive,
As they went or they returned,
At the house where these sojourned.
Sometimes their strong speed they slacken,
Though they are not overtaken;
In sleep their jubilant troop is near,—
I tuneful voices overhear;
It may be in wood or waste,—
At unawares 'tis come and past.

Their near camp my spirit knows
By signs gracious as rainbows.
I thenceforward, and long after,
Listen for their harplike laughter,
And carry in my heart, for days,
Peace that hallows rudest ways.

## Two Rivers

Thy summer voice, Musketaquit,
Repeats the music of the rain;
But sweeter rivers pulsing flit
Through thee, as thou through Concord Plain.

Thou in thy narrow banks art pent:
The stream I love unbounded goes
Through flood and sea and firmament;
Through light, through life, it forward flows.

I see the inundation sweet,
I hear the spending of the stream
Through years, through men, through Nature fleet,
Through love and thought, through power and dream.

Musketaquit, a goblin strong,
Of shard and flint makes jewels gay;
They lose their grief who hear his song,
And where he winds is the day of day.

So forth and brighter fares my stream,—
Who drink it shall not thirst again;
No darkness stains its equal gleam
And ages drop in it like rain.

## The Apology

Think me not unkind and rude
    That I walk alone in grove and glen;
I go to the god of the wood
    To fetch his word to men.

Tax not my sloth that I
    Fold my arms beside the brook;
Each cloud that floated in the sky
    Writes a letter in my book.

Chide me not, laborious band,
    For the idle flowers I brought;
Every aster in my hand
    Goes home loaded with a thought.

There was never mystery
    But 'tis figured in the flowers;
Was never secret history
    But birds tell it in the bowers.

One harvest from thy field
    Homeward brought the oxen strong;
A second crop thine acres yield,
    Which I gather in a song.

## Days

Daughters of Time, the hypocritic Days,
Muffled and dumb like barefoot dervishes,
And marching single in an endless file,
Bring diadems and fagots in their hands.
To each they offer gifts after his will,
Bread, kingdoms, stars, and sky that holds them all.
I, in my pleached garden, watched the pomp,
Forgot my morning wishes, hastily
Took a few herbs and apples, and the Day
Turned and departed silent. I, too late,
Under her solemn fillet saw the scorn.

## Bacchus

Bring me wine, but wine which never grew
In the belly of the grape,
Or grew on vine whose tap-roots, reaching through
Under the Andes to the Cape,
Suffered no savour of the earth to scape.

Let its grapes the morn salute
From a nocturnal root,
Which feels the acrid juice
Of Styx and Erebus;
And turns the woe of Night,
By its own craft, to a more rich delight.

We buy ashes for bread;
We buy diluted wine;
Give me of the true,—
Whose ample leaves and tendrils curled
Among the silver hills of heaven,
Draw everlasting dew;

Wine of wine,
Blood of the world,
Form of forms, and mould of statures,
That I intoxicated,
And by the draught assimilated,
May float at pleasure through all natures;
The bird-language rightly spell,
And that which roses say so well.
Wine that is shed
Like the torrents of the sun
Up the horizon walls,
Or like the Atlantic streams, which run
When the South Sea calls.

Water and bread,
Food which needs no transmuting,
Rainbow-flowering, wisdom-fruiting
Wine which is already man,
Food which teach and reason can.

Wine which Music is,—
Music and wine are one,—
That I, drinking this,
Shall hear far Chaos talk with me;
Kings unborn shall walk with me;
And the poor grass shall plot and plan
What it will do when it is man.
Quickened so, will I unlock
Every crypt of every rock.

I thank the joyful juice
For all I know;—
Winds of remembering
Of the ancient being blow,
And seeming-solid walls of use
Open and flow.

Pour, Bacchus! the remembering wine;
Retrieve the loss of me and mine!
Vine for vine be antidote,
And the grape requite the lote!
Haste to cure the old despair,—
Reason in Nature's lotus drenched,
The memory of ages quenched;
Give them again to shine;
Let wine repair what this undid;
And where the infection slid,
A dazzling memory revive;
Refresh the faded tints,
Recut the aged prints,
And write my old adventures with the pen
Which on the first day drew,
Upon the tablets blue,
The dancing Pleiads and eternal men.

### Give All to Love

Give all to love;
Obey thy heart;
Friends, kindred, days,
Estate, good-fame,
Plans, credit, and the Muse,—
Nothing refuse.

'Tis a brave master;
Let it have scope:
Follow it utterly,
Hope beyond hope:
High and more high
It dives into noon,
With wing unspent,
Untold intent;

But it is a god,
Knows its own path,
And the outlets of the sky.

It was never for the mean;
It requireth courage stout,
Souls above doubt,
Valor unbending;
It will reward,—
They shall return
More than they were,
And ever ascending

Leave all for love;
Yet, hear me, yet,
One word more thy heart behoved,
One pulse.more of firm endeavor,—
Keep thee to-day
To-morrow, forever,
Free as an Arab
Of thy beloved.

Cling with life to the maid;
But when the surprise,
First vague shadow of surmise
Flits across her bosom young
Of a joy apart from thee,
Free be she, fancy-free;
Nor thou detain her vesture's hem,
Nor the palest rose she flung
From her summer diadem.

Though thou loved her as thyself,
As a self of purer clay,
Though her parting dims the day,

Stealing grace from all alive;
Heartily know,
When half-gods go,
The gods arrive.

### Uriel

It fell in the ancient periods
    Which the brooding soul surveys,
Or ever the wild Time coined itself
    Into calendar months and days.

This was the lapse of Uriel,
Which in Paradise befell.
Once, among the Pleiads walking,
Seyd overheard the young gods talking;
And the treason, too long pent,
To his ears was evident.
The young deities discussed
Laws of form, and metre just,
Orb, quintessence, and sunbeams,
What subsisteth, and what seems.
One, with low tones that decide,
And doubt and reverend use defied,
With a look that solved the sphere,
And stirred the devils everywhere,
Gave his sentiment divine
Against the being of a line.
'Line in nature is not found;
Unit and universe are round;
In vain produced, all rays return;
Evil will bless, and ice will burn.'
As Uriel spoke with piercing eye,
A shudder ran around the sky;
The stern old war-gods shook their heads,
The seraphs frowned from myrtle-beds;

Seemed to the holy festival
The rash word boded ill to all;
The balance-beam of Fate was bent;
The bounds of good and ill were rent;
Strong Hades could not keep his own,
But all slid to confusion.

A sad self-knowledge, withering, fell
On the beauty of Uriel;
In heaven once eminent, the god
Withdrew, that hour, into his cloud;
Whether doomed to long gyration
In the sea of generation,
Or by knowledge grown too bright
To hit the nerve of feebler sight.
Straightway, a forgetting wind
Stole over the celestial kind,
And their lips the secret kept,
If in ashes and fire-seed slept.
But now and then, truth-speaking things
Shamed the angels' veiling wings;
And, shrilling from the solar course,
Or from fruit of chemic force,
Procession of a soul in matter,
Or the speeding change of water,
Or out of the good of evil born,
Came Uriel's voice of cherub scorn,
And a blush tinged the upper sky,
And the gods shook, they knew not why.

## Good-bye

Good-bye, proud world! I'm going home:
Thou art not my friend, and I'm not thine.
Long through thy weary crowds I roam;
A river-ark on the ocean brine,
Long I've been tossed like the driven foam;
But now, proud world! I'm going home.

Good-bye to Flattery's fawning face;
To Grandeur with his wise grimace;
To upstart Wealth's averted eye;
To supple Office, low and high;
To crowded halls, to court and street;
To frozen hearts and hasting feet;
To those who go, and those who come;
Good-bye, proud world! I'm going home

I am going to my own hearth-stone,
Bosomed in yon green hills alone,—
A secret nook in a pleasant land,
Whose groves the frolic fairies planned;
Where arches green, the livelong day,
Echo the blackbird's roundelay,
And vulgar feet have never trod
A spot that is sacred to thought and God.

O, when I am safe in my sylvan home,
I tread on the pride of Greece and Rome;
And when I am stretched beneath the pines,
Where the evening star so holy shines,
I laugh at the lore and the pride of man,
At the sophist schools, and the learned clan;
For what are they all, in their high conceit,
When man in the bush with God may meet?

## History

There is no great and no small
To the Soul that maketh all:
And where it cometh, all things are;
And it cometh every where.

I am owner of the sphere,
Of the seven stars and the solar year,
Of Caesar's hand, and Plato's brain,
Of Lord Christ's heart, and Shakespeare's strain.

## Brahma

If the red slayer think he slays,
    Or if the slain think he is slain,
They know not well the subtle ways
    I keep, and pass, and turn again.

Far or forgot to me is near;
    Shadow and sunlight are the same;
The vanquished gods to me appear;
    And one to me are shame and fame.

They reckon ill who leave me out;
    When me they fly, I am the wings;
I am the doubter and the doubt,
    And I the hymn the Brahmin sings.

The strong gods pine for my abode,
    And pine in vain the sacred Seven;
But thou, meek lover of the good!
    Find me, and turn thy back on heaven.

## Concord Hymn

SUNG AT THE COMPLETION OF THE CONCORD MONUMENT,
APRIL 19, 1836

By the rude bridge that arched the flood,
    Their flag to April's breeze unfurled,
Here once the embattled farmers stood,
    And fired the shot heard round the world.

The foe long since in silence slept;
    Alike the conqueror silent sleeps;
And Time the ruined bridge has swept
    Down the dark stream which seaward creeps.

On this green bank, by this soft stream,
    We set to-day a votive stone;
That memory may their deed redeem,
    When, like our sires, our sons are gone.

Spirit, that made those heroes dare
    To die, or leave their children free,
Bid Time and Nature gently spare
    The shaft we raise to them and thee.

CHARLES FENNO HOFFMAN                    1806–1884

## Monterey

We were not many,—we who stood
 Before the iron sleet that day;
Yet many a gallant spirit would
Give half his years if but he could
 Have been with us at Monterey.

Now here, now there, the shot it hailed
 In deadly drifts of fiery spray,
Yet not a single soldier quailed
When wounded comrades round them wailed
 Their dying shout at Monterey.

And on, still on our column kept,
 Through walls of flame, its withering way;
Where fell the dead, the living stept,
Still charging on the guns which swept
 The slippery streets of Monterey.

The foe himself recoiled aghast,
 When, striking where he strongest lay,
We swooped his flanking batteries past,
And, braving full their murderous blast,
 Stormed home the towers of Monterey.

Our banners on those turrets wave,
 And there our evening bugles play;
Where orange boughs above their grave,
Keep green the memory of the brave
 Who fought and fell at Monterey.

We are not many,—we who pressed
 Beside the brave who fell that day;
But who of us has not confessed
He'd rather share their warrior rest
 Than not have been at Monterey?

# HENRY WADSWORTH LONGFELLOW    1807–1882

## A Psalm of Life

### WHAT THE HEART OF THE YOUNG MAN
### SAID TO THE PSALMIST

Tell me not, in mournful numbers,
 Life is but an empty dream!
For the soul is dead that slumbers,
 And things are not what they seem.

Life is real! Life is earnest!
 And the grave is not its goal;
Dust thou art, to dust returnest,
 Was not spoken of the soul.

Not enjoyment, and not sorrow,
 Is our destined end or way;
But to act, that each to-morrow
 Find us farther than to-day.

Art is long, and Time is fleeting,
 And our hearts, though stout and brave,
Still, like muffled drums, are beating
 Funeral marches to the grave.

In the world's broad field of battle,
 In the bivouac of Life,
Be not like dumb, driven cattle!
 Be a hero in the strife!

Trust no Future, howe'er pleasant!
 Let the dead Past bury its dead!
Act,—act in the living Present!
 Heart within, and God o'erhead!

Lives of great men all remind us
 We can make our lives sublime,
And, departing leave behind us
 Footprints on the sands of time;—

Footprints, that perhaps another,
 Sailing o'er life's solemn main,
A forlorn and shipwrecked brother,
 Seeing, shall take heart again.

Let us, then, be up and doing,
 With a heart for any fate;
Still achieving, still pursuing,
 Learn to labor and to wait.

## My Cathedral

Like two cathedral towers these stately pines
 Uplift their fretted summits tipped with cones;
 The arch beneath them is not built with stones—
Not Art but Nature traced these lovely lines,
And carved this graceful arabesque of vines;
 No organ but the wind here sighs and moans,
 No sepulchre conceals a martyr's bones,
No marble bishop on his tomb reclines.
Enter! the pavement, carpeted with leaves,
 Gives back a softened echo to thy tread!
 Listen! the choir is singing; all the birds,
In leafy galleries beneath the eaves,
 Are singing! listen, ere the sound be fled,
 And learn there may be worship without words.

## The Arrow and the Song

I shot an arrow into the air,
It fell to earth, I know not where;
For, so swiftly it flew, the sight
Could not follow it in its flight.

I breathed a song into the air,
It fell to earth, I know not where;
For who has sight so keen and strong
That it can follow the flight of song?

Long, long afterward, in an oak
I found the arrow, still unbroke;
And the song, from beginning to end,
I found again in the heart of a friend.

## The Rainy Day

The day is cold, and dark, and dreary;
It rains, and the wind is never weary;
The vine still clings to the mouldering wall,
But at every gust the dead leaves fall,
    And the day is dark and dreary.

My life is cold, and dark, and dreary;
It rains, and the wind is never weary;
My thoughts still cling to the mouldering Past,
But the hopes of youth fall thick in the blast,
    And the days are dark and dreary.

Be still, sad heart! and cease repining;
Behind the clouds is the sun still shining;
Thy fate is the common fate of all,
Into each life some rain must fall,
    Some days must be dark and dreary.

## *Daybreak*

A wind came up out of the sea,
And said, "O mists, make room for me!"

It hailed the ships, and cried, "Sail on,
Ye mariners, the night is gone!"

And hurried landward far away,
Crying, "Awake! it is the day!"

It said unto the forest, "Shout!
Hang all your leafy banners out!"

It touched the wood-bird's folded wing,
And said, "O bird, awake and sing!"

And o'er the farms, "O chanticleer,
Your clarion blow; the day is near!"

It whispered to the fields of corn,
"Bow down, and hail the coming morn!"

It shouted through the belfry-tower,
"Awake, O bell! proclaim the hour."

It crossed the churchyard with a sigh,
And said, "Not yet! in quiet lie."

## The Village Blacksmith

Under a spreading chestnut-tree
    The village smithy stands;
The smith, a mighty man is he,
    With large and sinewy hands;
And the muscles of his brawny arms
    Are strong as iron bands.

His hair is crisp and black and long;
    His face is like the tan;
His brow is wet with honest sweat,—
    He earns whate'er he can,
And looks the whole world in the face,
    For he owes not any man.

Week in, week out, from morn till night,
    You can hear his bellows blow;
You can hear him swing his heavy sledge,
    With measured beat and slow,
Like a sexton ringing the village bell,
    When the evening sun is low.

And children coming home from school,
    Look in at the open door;
They love to see the flaming forge,
    And hear the bellows roar,
And catch the burning sparks that fly
    Like chaff from the threshing-floor.

He goes on Sunday to the church,
    And sits among his boys;
He hears the parson pray and preach;
    He hears his daughter's voice,
Singing in the village choir,
    And it makes his heart rejoice.

It sounds to him like her mother's voice,
　　Singing in Paradise!
He needs must think of her once more,
　　How in the grave she lies;
And with his hard, rough hand he wipes
　　A tear out of his eyes.

Toiling, rejoicing, sorrowing,
　　Onward through life he goes;
Each morning sees some task begin,
　　Each evening sees it close;
Something attempted, something done,
　　Has earned a night's repose.

Thanks, thanks to thee, my worthy friend,
　　For the lesson thou hast taught!
Thus at the flaming forge of life
　　Our fortunes must be wrought;
Thus on its sounding anvil shaped
　　Each burning deed and thought!

### *Nature*

As a fond mother, when the day is o'er,
　　Leads by the hand her little child to bed,
　　Half willing, half reluctant to be led,
And leave his broken playthings on the floor,
Still gazing at them through the open door,
　　Nor wholly reassured and comforted
　　By promises of others in their stead,
Which, though more splendid, may not please him more;
So Nature deals with us, and takes away
　　Our playthings one by one, and by the hand
　　Leads us to rest so gently, that we go
Scarce knowing if we wish to go or stay,
　　Being too full of sleep to understand
　　How far the unknown transcends the what we know.

## Hymn to the Night

'Ασπασίη, τρίλλιστος

I heard the trailing garments of the Night
    Sweep through her marble halls!
I saw her sable skirts all fringed with light
    From the celestial walls!

I felt her presence, by its spell of might,
    Stoop o'er me from above;
The calm, majestic presence of the Night,
    As of the one I love.

I heard the sounds of sorrow and delight,
    The manifold, soft chimes,
That fill the haunted chambers of the Night,
    Like some old poet's rhymes.

From the cool cisterns of the midnight air
    My spirit drank repose;
The fountain of perpetual peace flows there,—
    From those deep cisterns flows.

O holy Night! from thee I learn to bear
    What man has borne before!
Thou layest thy finger on the lips of Care,
    And they complain no more.

Peace! Peace! Orestes-like I breathe this prayer!
    Descend with broad-winged flight,
The welcome, the thrice-prayed-for, the most fair,
    The best-beloved Night!

## Milton

I pace the sounding sea-beach and behold
How the voluminous billows roll and run,
Upheaving and subsiding, while the sun
Shines through their sheeted emerald far unrolled
And the ninth wave, slow gathering fold on fold
All its loose-flowing garments into one,
Plunges upon the shore, and floods the dun
Pale reach of sands, and changes them to gold.
So in majestic cadence rise and fall
The mighty undulations of thy song,
O sightless bard, England's Maeonides!
And ever and anon, high over all
Uplifted, a ninth wave superb and strong,
Floods all the soul with its melodious seas.

## Chaucer

An old man in a lodge within a park;
The chamber walls depicted all around
With portraitures of huntsman, hawk, and hound,
And the hurt deer. He listeneth to the lark,
Whose song comes with the sunshine through the dark
Of painted glass in leaden lattice bound;
He listeneth and he laugheth at the sound,
Then writeth in a book like any clerk.
He is the poet of the dawn, who wrote
The Canterbury Tales, and his old age
Made beautiful with song; and as I read
I hear the crowing cock, I hear the note
Of lark and linnet, and from every page
Rise odors of plowed field or flowery mead.

### The Discoverer of the North Cape

Othere, the old sea-captain,
  Who dwelt in Helgoland,
To King Alfred, the Lover of Truth,
Brought a snow-white walrus-tooth,
  Which he held in his brown right hand.

His figure was tall and stately;
  Like a boy's his eye appeared;
His hair was yellow as hay,
But threads of a silvery gray
  Gleamed in his tawny beard.

Hearty and hale was Othere,
  His cheek had the color of oak;
With a kind of laugh in his speech,
Like the sea-tide on a beach,
  As unto the King he spoke.

And Alfred, King of the Saxons,
  Had a book upon his knees,
And wrote down the wondrous tale
Of him who was first to sail
  Into the Arctic seas.

"So far I live to the northward,
  No man lives north of me;
To the east are wild mountain-chains,
And beyond them meres and plains;
  To the westward all is sea.

"So far I live to the northward,
  From the harbor of Skeringes-hale,

If you only sailed by day,
With a fair wind all the way,
    More than a month would you sail.

"I own six hundred reindeer,
    With sheep and swine beside;
I have tribute from the Finns,
Whalebone and reindeer-skins,
    And ropes of walrus-hide.

"I ploughed the land with horses,
    But my heart was ill at ease,
For the old seafaring men
Came to me now and then,
    With their sagas of the seas;—

"Of Iceland and of Greenland,
    And the stormy Hebrides,
And the undiscovered deep;—
Oh, I could not eat nor sleep
    For thinking of those seas.

"To the northward stretched the desert,
    How far I fain would know;
So at last I sallied forth,
And three days sailed due north,
    As far as the whale-ships go.

"To the west of me was the ocean,
    To the right the desolate shore,
But I did not slacken sail
For the walrus or the whale,
    Till after three days more.

"The days grew longer and longer,
    Till they became as one,

And northward through the haze
I saw the sullen blaze
    Of the red midnight sun.

"And then uprose before me,
    Upon the water's edge,
The huge and haggard shape
Of that unknown North Cape,
    Whose form is like a wedge.

"The sea was rough and stormy,
    The tempest howled and wailed,
And the sea-fog, like a ghost,
Haunted that dreary coast,
    But onward still I sailed.

"Four days I steered to eastward,
    Four days without a night:
Round in a fiery ring
Went the great sun, O King,
    With red and lurid light."

Here Alfred, King of the Saxons,
    Ceased writing for a while;
And raised his eyes from his book,
With a strange and puzzled look,
    And an incredulous smile.

But Othere, the old sea-captain,
    He neither paused nor stirred,
Till the King listened, and then
Once more took up his pen,
    And wrote down every word.

"And now the land," said Othere,
    "Bent southward suddenly,

And I followed the curving shore
And ever southward bore
   Into a nameless sea.

"And there we hunted the walrus,
   The narwhale, and the seal;
Ha! 'twas a noble game!
And like the lightning's flame
   Flew our harpoons of steel.

"There were six of us all together,
   Norsemen of Helgoland;
In two days and no more
We killed of them threescore,
   And dragged them to the strand!"

Here Alfred, the Truth-teller,
   Suddenly closed his book,
And lifted his blue eyes,
With doubt and strange surmise
   Depicted in their look.

And Othere, the old sea-captain,
   Stared at him wild and weird,
Then smiled, till his shining teeth
Gleamed white from underneath
   His tawny, quivering beard.

And to the King of the Saxons,
   In witness of the truth,
Raising his noble head,
He stretched his brown hand, and said,
   "Behold this walrus-tooth!"

### A Dutch Picture

Simon Danz has come home again,
   From cruising about with his buccaneers;
He has singed the beard of the King of Spain
And carried away the Dean of Jaen
   And sold him in Algiers.

In his house by the Maese, with its roof of tiles,
   And weathercocks flying aloft in air,
There are silver tankards of antique styles,
Plunder of convent and castle, and piles
   Of carpets rich and rare.

In his tulip-garden there by the town,
   Overlooking the sluggish stream,
With his Moorish cap and dressing-gown,
The old sea-captain, hale and brown,
   Walks in a waking dream.

A smile in his gray mustachio lurks
   Whenever he thinks of the King of Spain,
And the listed tulips look like Turks,
And the silent gardener as he works
   Is changed to the Dean of Jaen.

The windmills on the outermost
   Verge of the landscape in the haze,
To him are towers on the Spanish coast,
With whiskered sentinels at their post,
   Though this is the river Maese.

But when the winter rains begin,
  He sits and smokes by the blazing brands,
And old seafaring men come in,
Goat-bearded, gray, and with double chin,
  And rings upon their hands.

They sit there in the shadow and shine
  Of the flickering fire of the winter night;
Figures in color and design
Like those by Rembrandt of the Rhine,
  Half darkness and half light.

And they talk of ventures lost or won,
  And their talk is ever and ever the same,
While they drink the red wine of Tarragon,
From the cellars of some Spanish Don,
  Or convent set on flame.

Restless at times, with heavy strides
  He paces his parlor to and fro;
He is like a ship that at anchor rides,
And swings with the rising and falling tides,
  And tugs at her anchor-tow.

Voices mysterious far and near,
  Sound of the wind and sound of the sea,
Are calling and whispering in his ear,
"Simon Danz! Why stayest thou here?
  Come forth and follow me!"

So he thinks he shall take to the sea again
  For one more cruise with his buccaneers,
To singe the beard of the King of Spain,
And capture another Dean of Jaen
  And sell him in Algiers.

## Snow-Flakes

Out of the bosom of the Air,
   Out of the cloud-folds of her garments shaken,
Over the woodlands brown and bare,
   Over the harvest-fields forsaken,
     Silent and soft and slow
     Descends the snow.

Even as our cloudy fancies take
   Suddenly shape in some divine expression,
Even as the troubled heart doth make
   In the white countenance confession,
     The troubled sky reveals
     The grief it feels.

This is the poem of the air,
   Slowly in silent syllables recorded;
This is the secret of despair,
   Long in its cloudy bosom hoarded,
     Now whispered and revealed
     To wood and field.

## The Tide Rises, the Tide Falls

The tide rises, the tide falls,
The twilight darkens, the curlew calls;
Along the sea-sands damp and brown
The traveller hastens toward the town,
    And the tide rises, the tide falls.

Darkness settles on roofs and walls,
But the sea, the sea in the darkness calls;
The little waves, with their soft, white hands,

Efface the footprints in the sands,
    And the tide rises, the tide falls.

The morning breaks; the steeds in their stalls
Stamp and neigh, as the hostler calls;
The day returns, but nevermore
Returns the traveller to the shore,
    And the tide rises, the tide falls.

## God's-Acre

I like that ancient Saxon phrase which calls
    The burial-ground God's-Acre! It is just;
It consecrates each grave within its walls,
    And breathes a benison o'er the sleeping dust.

God's-Acre! Yes, that blessed name imparts
    Comfort to those who in the grave have sown
The seed that they had garnered in their hearts,
    Their bread of life, alas! no more their own.

Into its furrows shall we all be cast,
    In the sure faith that we shall rise again
At the great harvest, when the archangel's blast
    Shall winnow, like a fan, the chaff and grain.

Then shall the good stand in immortal bloom,
    In the fair gardens of that second birth;
And each bright blossom mingle its perfume
    With that of flowers which never bloomed on earth.

With thy rude ploughshare, Death, turn up the sod,
    And spread the furrow for the seed we sow;
This is the field and Acre of our God,
    This is the place where human harvests grow!

### The Cumberland

At anchor in Hampton Roads we lay,
  On board of the Cumberland, sloop-of-war;
And at times from the fortress across the bay
    The alarum of drums swept past,
    Or a bugle blast
  From the camp on the shore.

Then far away to the south uprose
  A little feather of snow-white smoke,
And we knew that the iron ship of our foes
    Was steadily steering its course
    To try the force
  Of our ribs of oak.

Down upon us heavily runs,
  Silent and sullen, the floating fort;
Then comes a puff of smoke from her guns,
    And leaps the terrible death,
    With fiery breath,
  From each open port.

We are not idle, but send her straight
  Defiance back in a full broadside!
As hail rebounds from a roof of slate,
    Rebounds our heavier hail
    From each iron scale
  Of the monster's hide.

"Strike your flag!" the rebel cries
  In his arrogant old plantation strain.
"Never!" our gallant Morris replies:

"It is better to sink than to yield!"
And the whole air pealed
With the cheers of our men.

Then, like a kraken huge and black,
She crushed our ribs in her iron grasp!
Down went the Cumberland all a wrack,
With a sudden shudder of death,
And the cannon's breath
For her dying gasp.

Next morn, as the sun rose over the bay,
Still floated our flag at the mainmast head.
Lord, how beautiful was Thy day!
Every waft of the air
Was a whisper of prayer,
Or a dirge for the dead.

Ho! brave hearts that went down in the seas!
Ye are at peace in the troubled stream;
Ho! brave land! with hearts like these,
Thy flag, that is rent in twain,
Shall be one again,
And without a seam!

## Ship of State

### FROM "THE BUILDING OF THE SHIP"

Thou, too, sail on, O Ship of State!
Sail on, O Union, strong and great!
Humanity with all its fears,
With all its hopes of future years,
Is hanging breathless on thy fate!
We know what Master laid thy keel,
What Workmen wrought thy ribs of steel,
Who made each mast, and sail, and rope,
What anvils rang, what hammers beat,
In what a forge and what a heat
Were shaped the anchors of thy hope!
Fear not each sudden sound and shock,
'Tis of the wave and not the rock;
'Tis but the flapping of the sail,
And not a rent made by the gale!
In spite of rock and tempest's roar,
In spite of false lights on the shore,
Sail on, nor fear to breast the sea!
Our hearts, our hopes, are all with thee,
Our hearts, our hopes, our prayers, our tears,
Our faith, triumphant o'er our fears,
Are all with thee,—are all with thee!

# JOHN GREENLEAF WHITTIER 1807–1892

## *Ichabod*

### DANIEL WEBSTER. 1850

So fallen! so lost! the light withdrawn,
    Which once he wore!
The glory from his gray hairs gone
    Forevermore!

Revile him not,—the Tempter hath
    A snare for all!
And pitying tears, not scorn and wrath,
    Befit his fall!

O, dumb be passion's stormy rage,
    When he who might
Have lighted up and led his age
    Falls back in night!

Scorn! would the angels laugh to mark
    A bright soul driven,
Fiend-goaded, down the endless dark,
    From hope and heaven?

Let not the land, once proud of him,
    Insult him now;
Nor brand with deeper shame his dim,
    Dishonored brow.

But let its humbled sons instead,
    From sea to lake,
A long lament, as for the dead,
    In sadness make.

Of all we loved and honored, naught
    Save power remains,—
A fallen angel's pride of thought,
    Still strong in chains.

All else is gone; from those great eyes
    The soul has fled:
When faith is lost, when honor dies,
    The man is dead!

Then pay the reverence of old days
    To his dead fame;
Walk backward, with averted gaze,
    And hide the shame!

## The Reformer

All grim and soiled and brown with tan,
    I saw a Strong One, in his wrath,
Smiting the godless shrines of man
    Along his path.

The Church beneath her trembling dome
    Essayed in vain her ghostly charm:
Wealth shook within his gilded home
    With strange alarm.

Fraud from his secret chambers fled
    Before the sunlight bursting in:
Sloth drew her pillow o'er her head
    To drown the din.

"Spare," Art implored, "yon holy pile;
    That grand old time-worn turret spare:"
Meek Reverence, kneeling in the aisle,
    Cried out, "Forbear!"

Gray-bearded Use, who, deaf and blind,
　　Groped for his old accustomed stone,
Leaned on his staff, and wept to find
　　　　His seat o'erthrown.

Young Romance raised his dreamy eyes,
　　O'erhung with paly locks of gold,—
"Why smite," he asked in sad surprise,
　　　　"The fair, the old?"

Yet louder rang the Strong One's stroke,
　　Yet nearer flashed his axe's gleam;
Shuddering and sick of heart I woke,
　　　　As from a dream.

I looked: aside the dust-cloud rolled,—
　　The Waster seemed the Builder too;
Upspringing from the ruined Old
　　　　I saw the New.

'T was but the ruin of the bad,—
　　The wasting of the wrong and ill;
Whate'er of good the old time had
　　　　Was living still.

Calm grew the brows of him I feared;
　　The frown which awed me passed away,
And left behind a smile which cheered
　　　　Like breaking day.

The grain grew green on battle-plains,
　　O'er swarded war-mounds grazed the cow;
The slave stood forging from his chains
　　　　The spade and plough.

Where frowned the fort, pavilions gay
    And cottage windows, flower-entwined,
Looked out upon the peaceful bay
        And hills behind.

Through vine-wreathed cups with wine once red,
    The lights on brimming crystal fell,
Drawn, sparkling, from the rivulet head
        And mossy well.

Through prison-walls, like Heaven-sent hope,
    Fresh breezes blew, and sunbeams strayed,
And with the idle gallows-rope
        The young child played.

Where the doomed victim in his cell
    Had counted o'er the weary hours,
Glad school-girls, answering to the bell,
        Came crowned with flowers.

Grown wiser for the lesson given,
    I fear no longer, for I know
That where the share is deepest driven
        The best fruits grow.

The outworn rite, the old abuse,
    The pious fraud transparent grown,
The good held captive in the use
        Of wrong alone,—

These wait their doom, from that great law
    Which makes the past time serve to-day;
And fresher life the world shall draw
        From their decay.

O backward-looking son of time!
　　The new is old, the old is new,
The cycle of a change sublime
　　　　Still sweeping through.

So wisely taught the Indian seer;
　　Destroying Seva, forming Brahm,
Who wake by turn Earth's love and fear,
　　　　Are one, the same.

Idly as thou, in that old day
　　Thou mournest, did thy sire repine;
So, in his time, thy child grown gray
　　　　Shall sigh for thine.

But life shall on and upward go;
　　Th' eternal step of Progress beats
To that great anthem, calm and slow,
　　　　Which God repeats.

Take heart!—the Waster builds again,—
　　A charmèd like old Goodness hath;
The tares may perish,—but the grain
　　　　Is not for death.

God works in all things; all obey
　　His first propulsion from the night:
Wake thou and watch!—the world is gray
　　　　With morning light!

### Barbara Frietchie

Up from the meadows rich with corn,
Clear in the cool September morn,

The clustered spires of Frederick stand
Green-walled by the hills of Maryland.

Round about them orchards sweep,
Apple and peach tree fruited deep,

Fair as a garden of the Lord
To the eyes of the famished rebel horde,

On that pleasant morn of the early fall
When Lee marched over the mountain wall,—

Over the mountains, winding down,
Horse and foot into Frederick town.

Forty flags with their silver stars,
Forty flags with their crimson bars,

Flapped in the morning wind; the sun
Of noon looked down, and saw not one.

Up rose old Barbara Frietchie then,
Bowed with her fourscore years and ten;

Bravest of all in Frederick town,
She took up the flag the men hauled down;

In her attic-window the staff she set,
To show that one heart was loyal yet.

Up the street came the rebel tread,
Stonewall Jackson riding ahead.

Under his slouched hat left and right
He glanced: the old flag met his sight.

"Halt!"—the dust-brown ranks stood fast;
"Fire!"—out blazed the rifle-blast.

It shivered the window, pane and sash;
It rent the banner with seam and gash.

Quick, as it fell, from the broken staff
Dame Barbara snatched the silken scarf;

She leaned far out on the window-sill,
And shook it forth with a royal will.

"Shoot, if you must, this old gray head,
But spare your country's flag," she said.

A shade of sadness, a blush of shame,
Over the face of the leader came;

The nobler nature within him stirred
To life at that woman's deed and word:

"Who touches a hair of yon gray head
Dies like a dog! March on!" he said.

All day long through Frederick street
Sounded the tread of marching feet;

All day long that free flag tost
Over the heads of the rebel host.

Ever its torn folds rose and fell
On the loyal winds that loved it well;

And through the hill-gaps sunset light
Shone over it with a warm good-night.

Barbara Frietchie's work is o'er,
And the rebel rides on his raids no more.

Honor to her! and let a tear
Fall, for her sake, on Stonewall's bier.

Over Barbara Frietchie's grave,
Flag of freedom and union, wave!

Peace and order and beauty draw
Round thy symbol of light and law;

And ever the stars above look down
On thy stars below in Frederick town!

## Love of God

FROM "THE ETERNAL GOODNESS"

O friends! with whom my feet have trod
    The quiet aisles of prayer,
Glad witness to your zeal for God
    And love of man I bear.

I trace your lines of argument;
    Your logic linked and strong
I weigh as one who dreads dissent,
    And fears a doubt as wrong.

But still my human hands are weak
    To hold your iron creeds:
Against the words ye bid me speak
    My heart within me pleads.


Who fathoms the Eternal Thought?
    Who talks of scheme and plan?
The Lord is God! He needeth not
    The poor device of man.


I walk with bare, hushed feet the ground
    Ye tread with boldness shod;
I dare not fix with mete and bound
    The love and power of God.


Ye praise His justice; even such
    His pitying love I deem:
Ye seek a king; I fain would touch
    The robe that hath no seam.


Ye see the curse which overbroods
    A world of pain and loss;
I hear our Lord's beatitudes
    And prayer upon the cross.


More than your schoolmen teach, within
    Myself, alas! I know:
Too dark ye cannot paint the sin,
    Too small the merit show. . . .


I long for household voices gone,
    For vanished smiles I long,
But God hath led my dear ones on,
    And He can do no wrong.

I know not what the future hath
  Of marvel or surprise,
Assured alone that life and death
  His mercy underlies.

And if my heart and flesh are weak
  To bear an untried pain,
The bruisèd reed He will not break,
  But strengthen and sustain.

No offering of my own I have,
  Nor works my faith to prove;
I can but give the gifts He gave,
  And plead His love for love.

And so beside the Silent Sea
  I wait the muffled oar;
No harm from Him can come to me
  On ocean or on shore.

I know not where His islands lift
  Their fronded palms in air;
I only know I cannot drift
  Beyond His love and care.

O brothers! if my faith is vain,
  If hopes like these betray,
Pray for me that my feet may gain
  The sure and safer way.

And Thou, O Lord! by whom are seen
  Thy creatures as they be,
Forgive me if too close I lean
  My human heart on Thee!

## New England Winter

FROM "SNOW-BOUND"

The sun that brief December day
Rose cheerless over hills of gray,
And, darkly circled, gave at noon
A sadder light than waning moon.
Slow tracing down the thickening sky
Its mute and ominous prophecy,
A portent seeming less than threat,
It sank from sight before it set.
A chill no coat, however stout,
Of homespun stuff could quite shut out,
A hard, dull bitterness of cold,
That checked, mid-vein, the circling race
Of life-blood in the sharpened face,
The coming of the snow-storm told.
The wind blew east: we heard the roar
Of Ocean on his wintry shore,
And felt the strong pulse throbbing there
Beat with low rhythm our inland air.

Meanwhile we did our nightly chores,—
Brought in the wood from out of doors,
Littered the stalls, and from the mows
Raked down the herd's-grass for the cows;
Heard the horse whinnying for his corn;
And, sharply clashing horn on horn,
Impatient down the stanchion rows
The cattle shake their walnut bows;
While, peering from his early perch
Upon the scaffold's pole of birch,
The cock his crested helmet bent
And down his querulous challenge sent.

Unwarmed by any sunset light
The gray day darkened into night,
A night made hoary with the swarm
And whirl-dance of the blinding storm,
As zigzag wavering to and fro
Crossed and recrossed the wingèd snow:
And ere the early bedtime came
The white drift piled the window-frame,
And through the glass the clothes-line posts
Looked in like tall and sheeted ghosts.

So all night long the storm roared on:
The morning broke without a sun;
In tiny spherule traced with lines
Of Nature's geometric signs,
In starry flake, and pellicle,
All day the hoary meteor fell;
And, when the second morning shone,
We looked upon a world unknown,
On nothing we could call our own.
Around the glistening wonder bent
The blue walls of the firmament,
No cloud above, no earth below,—
A universe of sky and snow!
The old familiar sights of ours
Took marvellous shapes; strange domes and towers
Rose up where sty or corn-crib stood,
Or garden wall, or belt of wood;
A smooth white mound the brush-pile showed,
A fenceless drift what once was road;
The bridle-post an old man sat
With loose-flung coat and high cocked hat;
The well-curb had a Chinese roof;
And even the long sweep, high aloof,
In its slant splendor, seemed to tell
Of Pisa's leaning miracle.

A prompt, decisive man, no breath
Our father wasted: "Boys, a path!"
Well pleased, (for when did farmer boy
Count such a summons less than joy?)
Our buskins on our feet we drew;
With mittened hands, and caps drawn low,
To guard our necks and ears from snow,
We cut the solid whiteness through.
And, where the drift was deepest, made
A tunnel walled and overlaid
With dazzling crystal: we had read
Of rare Aladdin's wondrous cave,
And to our own his name we gave,
With many a wish the luck were ours
To test his lamp's supernal powers.
We reached the barn with merry din,
And roused the prisoned brutes within.
The old horse thrust his long head out,
And grave with wonder gazed about;
The cock his lusty greeting said,
And forth his speckled harem led;
The oxen lashed their tails, and hooked,
And mild reproach of hunger looked;
The hornèd patriarch of the sheep,
Like Egypt's Amun roused from sleep,
Shook his sage head with gesture mute,
And emphasized with stamp of foot.

All day the gusty north-wind bore
The loosening drift its breath before;
Low circling round its southern zone,
The sun through dazzling snow-mist shone.
No church-bell lent its Christian tone
To the savage air, no social smoke
Curled over woods of snow-hung oak.
A solitude made more intense

By dreary-voicèd elements,
The shrieking of the mindless wind,
The moaning tree-boughs swaying blind,
And on the glass the unmeaning beat
Of ghostly finger-tips of sleet.
Beyond the circle of our hearth
No welcome sound of toil or mirth
Unbound the spell, and testified
Of human life and thought outside.
We minded that the sharpest ear
The buried brooklet could not hear,
The music of whose liquid lip
Had been to us companionship,
And, in our lonely life, had grown
To have an almost human tone.

As night drew on, and, from the crest
Of wooded knolls that ridged the west,
The sun, a snow-blown traveller, sank
From sight beneath the smothering bank,
We piled, with care, our nightly stack
Of wood against the chimney-back,—
The oaken log, green, huge, and thick,
And on its top the stout back-stick;
The knotty forestick laid apart,
And filled between with curious art
The ragged brush; then, hovering near,
We watched the first red blaze appear,
Heard the sharp crackle, caught the gleam
On whitewashed wall and sagging beam,
Until the old, rude-furnished room
Burst, flower-like, into rosy bloom;
While radiant with a mimic flame
Outside the sparkling drift became,
And through the bare-boughed lilac-tree

Our own warm hearth seemed blazing free.
The crane and pendent trammels showed;
The Turks' heads on the andirons glowed;
While childish fancy, prompt to tell
The meaning of the miracle,
Whispered the old rhyme: *"Under the tree,*
*When fire outdoors burns merrily,*
*There the witches are making tea."*

The moon above the eastern wood
Shone at its full; the hill-range stood
Transfigured in the silver flood,
Its blown snows flashing cold and keen,
Dead white, save where some sharp ravine
Took shadow, or the sombre green
Of hemlocks turned to pitchy black
Against the whiteness at their back.
For such a world and such a night
Most fitting that unwarming light,
Which only seemed where'er it fell
To make the coldness visible.

Shut in from all the world without,
We sat the clean-winged hearth about,
Content to let the north-wind roar
In baffled rage at pane and door,
While the red logs before us beat
The frost-line back with tropic heat;
And ever, when a louder blast
Shook beam and rafter as it passed,
The merrier up its roaring draught
The great throat of the chimney laughed;
The house-dog on his paws outspread
Laid to the fire his drowsy head,
The cat's dark silhouette on the wall

A couchant tiger's seemed to fall;
And, for the winter fireside meet,
Between the andirons' straddling feet,
The mug of cider simmered slow,
The apples sputtered in a row,
And, close at hand, the basket stood
With nuts from brown October's wood.

## Laus Deo!

ON HEARING THE BELLS RING ON THE PASSAGE OF THE
CONSTITUTIONAL AMENDMENT ABOLISHING SLAVERY

It is done!
Clang of bell and roar of gun
Send the tidings up and down.
How the belfries rock and reel!
How the great guns, peal on peal,
Fling the joy from town to town!

Ring, O bells!
Every stroke exulting tells
Of the burial hour of crime.
Loud and long, that all may hear,
Ring for every listening ear
Of Eternity and Time!

Let us kneel:
God's own voice is in that peal,
And this spot is holy ground.
Lord, forgive us! What are we,
That our eyes this glory see,
That our ears have heard the sound!

For the Lord
On the whirlwind is abroad;

In the earthquake he has spoken;
  He has smitten with his thunder
  The iron walls asunder,
And the gates of brass are broken!

    Loud and long
  Lift the old exulting song;
Sing with Miriam by the sea:
  He has cast the mighty down;
  Horse and rider sink and drown;
He has triumphed gloriously!

    Did we dare,
 In our agony of prayer,
Ask for more than He has done?
  When was ever his right hand
  Over any time or land
Stretched as now beneath the sun?

    How they pale,
  Ancient myth and song and tale,
In this wonder of our days,
  When the cruel rod of war
  Blossoms white with righteous law,
And the wrath of man is praise!

    Blotted out!
  All within and all about
Shall a fresher life begin;
  Freer breathe the universe
  As it rolls its heavy curse
On the dead and buried sin.

    It is done!
  In the circuit of the sun
Shall the sound thereof go forth.

It shall bid the sad rejoice,
It shall give the dumb a voice,
It shall belt with joy the earth!

Ring and swing,
Bells of joy! On morning's wing
Send the song of praise abroad!
With a sound of broken chains,
Tell the nations that He reigns,
Who alone is Lord and God!

## The Trailing Arbutus

I wandered lonely where the pine-trees made
Against the bitter East their barricade,
    And, guided by its sweet
Perfume, I found, within a narrow dell,
The trailing spring flower tinted like a shell
    Amid dry leaves and mosses at my feet.

From under dead boughs, for whose loss the pines
Moaned ceaseless overhead, the blossoming vines
    Lifted their glad surprise,
While yet the bluebird smoothed in leafless trees
His feathers ruffled by the chill sea-breeze,
    And snow-drifts lingered under April skies.

As, pausing, o'er the lonely flower I bent,
I thought of lives thus lowly, clogged and pent,
    Which yet find room
Through care and cumber, coldness and decay,
To lend a sweetness to the ungenial day,
    And make the sad earth happier for their bloom.

## The Waiting

I wait and watch: before my eyes
   Methinks the night grows thin and gray;
I wait and watch the eastern skies
To see the golden spears uprise
   Beneath the oriflamme of day!

Like one whose limbs are bound in trance
   I hear the day-sounds swell and grow,
And see across the twilight glance,
Troop after troop, in swift advance,
   The shining ones with plumes of snow!

I know the errand of their feet,
   I know what mighty work is theirs;
I can but lift up hands unmeet
The threshing-floors of God to beat,
   And speed them with unworthy prayers.

I will not dream in vain despair
   The steps of progress wait for me:
The puny leverage of a hair
The planet's impulse well may spare,
   A drop of dew the tided sea.

The loss, if loss there be, is mine,
   And yet not mine if understood;
For one shall grasp and one resign,
One drink life's rue, and one its wine,
   And God shall make the balance good.

O power to do! O baffled will!
   O prayer and action! ye are one.
Who may not strive, may yet fulfil
The harder task of standing still,
   And good but wished with God is done!

EDGAR ALLAN POE                                    1809–1849

## The Haunted Palace

FROM "THE FALL OF THE HOUSE OF USHER"

In the greenest of our valleys
  By good angels tenanted,
Once a fair and stately palace—
  Radiant palace—reared its head.
In the monarch Thought's dominion—
  It stood there!
Never seraph spread a pinion
  Over fabric half so fair!

Banners yellow, glorious, golden,
  On its roof did float and flow,
(This—all this—was in the olden
  Time long ago),
And every gentle air that dallied,
  In that sweet day,
Along the ramparts plumed and pallid,
  A winged odor went away.

Wanderers in that happy valley,
  Through two luminous windows, saw
Spirits moving musically,
  To a lute's well-tuned law,
Round about a throne where, sitting,
  (Porphyrogene!)
In state his glory well befitting,
  The ruler of the realm was seen.

And all with pearl and ruby glowing
  Was the fair palace door,
Through which came flowing, flowing, flowing,
  And sparkling evermore,

A troop of Echoes, whose sweet duty
 Was but to sing,
In voices of surpassing beauty,
 The wit and wisdom of their king.

But evil things, in robes of sorrow,
 Assailed the monarch's high estate.
(Ah, let us mourn!—for never morrow
 Shall dawn upon him, desolate!)
And round about his home the glory
 That blushed and bloomed,
Is but a dim-remembered story
 Of the old time entombed.

And travellers, now, within that valley,
 Through the red-litten windows see
Vast forms, that move fantastically
 To a discordant melody,
While, like a ghastly rapid river,
 Through the pale door
A hideous throng rush out forever
 And laugh—but smile no more.

### To Helen

Helen, thy beauty is to me
 Like those Nicéan barks of yore,
That gently, o'er a perfumed sea,
 The weary, way-worn wanderer bore
 To his own native shore.

On desperate seas long wont to roam,
 Thy hyacinth hair, thy classic face,
Thy Naiad airs have brought me home
 To the glory that was Greece,
 And the grandeur that was Rome.

Lo! in yon brilliant window-niche
　How statue-like I see thee stand,
The agate lamp within thy hand!
　Ah, Psyche, from the regions which
　Are Holy-Land!


## A Dream within a Dream

Take this kiss upon thy brow!
And, in parting from you now,
Thus much let me avow—
You are not wrong, to deem
That my days have been a dream;
Yet if Hope has flown away
In a night, or in a day,
In a vision, or in none,
Is it therefore the less *gone*?
*All* that we see or seem
Is but a dream within a dream.

I stand amid the roar
Of a surf-tormented shore,
And I hold within my hand
Grains of the golden sand—
How few! yet how they creep
Through my fingers to the deep,
While I weep—while I weep!

O God! can I not grasp
Them with a tighter clasp?
O God! can I not save
*One* from the pitiless wave?
Is *all* that we see or seem
But a dream within a dream?

## Israfel

And the angel Israfel, whose heart-strings are a lute, and who
has the sweetest voice of all God's creatures.—KORAN.

In Heaven a spirit doth dwell
    "Whose heart-strings are a lute";
None sing so wildly well
As the angel Israfel,
And the giddy stars (so legends tell)
Ceasing their hymns, attend the spell
    Of his voice, all mute.

Tottering above
    In her highest noon,
    The enamored Moon
Blushes with love,
    While, to listen, the red levin
    (With the rapid Pleiads, even,
    Which were seven,)
    Pauses in Heaven.

And they say (the starry choir
    And the other listening things)
That Israfeli's fire
Is owing to that lyre
    By which he sits and sings—
The trembling living wire
    Of those unusual strings.

But the skies that angel trod,
    Where deep thoughts are a duty,
Where Love's a grown-up God,
    Where the Houri glances are
Imbued with all the beauty
    Which we worship in a star.

Therefore, thou art not wrong,
  Israfeli, who despisest
An unimpassioned song;
To thee the laurels belong,
  Best bard, because the wisest!
Merrily live, and long!

The ecstasies above
  With thy burning measures suit—
Thy grief, thy joy, thy hate, thy love,
  With the fervor of thy lute—
  Well may the stars be mute!

Yes, Heaven is thine; but this
  Is a world of sweets and sours;
  Our flowers are merely—flowers,
And the shadow of thy perfect bliss
  Is the sunshine of ours.

If I could dwell
Where Israfel
  Hath dwelt, and he where I,
He might not sing so wildly well
  A mortal melody,
While a bolder note than this might swell
  From my lyre within the sky.

## The City in the Sea

Lo! Death has reared himself a throne
In a strange city lying alone
Far down within the dim West,
Where the good and the bad and the worst and the best
Have gone to their eternal rest.
There shrines and palaces and towers
(Time-eaten towers that tremble not!)

Resemble nothing that is ours.
Around, by lifting winds forgot,
Resignedly beneath the sky
The melancholy waters lie.

No rays from the holy heaven come down
On the long night-time of that town;
But light from out the lurid sea
Streams up the turrets silently—
Gleams up the pinnacles far and free—
Up domes—up spires—up kingly halls—
Up fanes—up Babylon-like walls—
Up shadowy long-forgotten bowers
Of sculptured ivy and stone flowers—
Up many and many a marvelous shrine
Whose wreathed friezes intertwine
The viol, the violet, and the vine.

Resignedly beneath the sky
The melancholy waters lie.
So blend the turrets and shadows there
That all seem pendulous in air,
While from a proud tower in the town
Death looks gigantically down.

There open fanes and gaping graves
Yawn level with the luminous waves;
But not the riches there that lie
In each idol's diamond eye—
Not the gaily-jeweled dead
Tempt the waters from their bed;
For no ripples curl, alas!
Along that wilderness of glass—
No swellings tell that winds may be
Upon some far-off happier sea—
No heavings hint that winds have been
On seas less hideously serene.

But lo, a stir is in the air!
The wave—there is a movement there!
As if the towers had thrust aside,
In slightly sinking, the dull tide—
As if their tops had feebly given
A void within the filmy Heaven.

The waves have now a redder glow—
The hours are breathing faint and low—
And when, amid no earthly moans,
Down, down that town shall settle hence,
Hell, rising from a thousand thrones,
Shall do it reverence.

## To One in Paradise

Thou wast all that to me, love,
   For which my soul did pine—
A green isle in the sea, love,
   A fountain and a shrine,
All wreathed with fairy fruits and flowers,
   And all the flowers were mine.

Ah, dream too bright to last!
   Ah, starry Hope! that didst arise
But to be overcast!
   A voice from out the Future cries,
"On! on!"—but o'er the Past
   (Dim gulf!) my spirit hovering lies
Mute, motionless, aghast!

For, alas! alas! with me
   The light of Life is o'er!
No more—no more—no more—
   (Such language holds the solemn sea
To the sands upon the shore)

Shall bloom the thunder-blasted tree,
Or the stricken eagle soar!

And all my days are trances,
And all my nightly dreams
Are where thy gray eye glances,
And where thy footstep gleams—
In what ethereal dances,
By what eternal streams.

## Annabel Lee

It was many and many a year ago,
In a kingdom by the sea,
That a maiden there lived whom you may know
By the name of Annabel Lee;—
And this maiden she lived with no other thought
Than to love and be loved by me.

She was a child and I was a child,
In this kingdom by the sea,
But we loved with a love that was more than love—
I and my Annabel Lee—
With a love that the winged seraphs of Heaven
Coveted her and me.

And this was the reason that, long ago,
In this kingdom by the sea,
A wind blew out of a cloud, by night
Chilling my Annabel Lee;
So that her highborn kinsmen came
And bore her away from me,
To shut her up in a sepulchre
In this kingdom by the sea.

The angels, not half so happy in Heaven,
  Went envying her and me:
Yes! that was the reason (as all men know,
  In this kingdom by the sea)
That the wind came out of the cloud, chilling
  And killing my Annabel Lee.

But our love it was stronger by far than the love
  Of those who were older than we—
  Of many far wiser than we—
And neither the angels in Heaven above
  Nor the demons down under the sea,
Can ever dissever my soul from the soul
  Of the beautiful Annabel Lee:—

For the moon never beams without bringing me dreams
  Of the beautiful Annabel Lee;
And the stars never rise but I see the bright eyes
  Of the beautiful Annabel Lee;
And so, all the night-tide, I lie down by the side
Of my darling, my darling, my life and my bride,
  In her sepulchre there by the sea—
  In her tomb by the sounding sea.

## Romance

Romance, who loves to nod and sing,
With drowsy head and folded wing,
Among the green leaves as they shake
Far down within some shadowy lake,
To me a painted paroquet
Hath been—a most familiar bird—
Taught me my alphabet to say—
To lisp my very earliest word
While in the wild wood I did lie,
A child—with a most knowing eye.

Of late, eternal condor years
So shake the very Heaven on high
With tumult as they thunder by,
I have no time for idle cares
Through gazing on the unquiet sky.
And when an hour with calmer wings
Its down upon my spirit flings—
That little time with lyre and rhyme
To while away—forbidden things!
My heart would feel to be a crime
Unless it trembled with the strings.

## Ulalume

The skies they were ashen and sober;
    The leaves they were crisped and sere—
    The leaves they were withering and sere;
It was night in the lonesome October
    Of my most immemorial year;
It was hard by the dim lake of Auber,
    In the misty mid region of Weir—
It was down by the dank tarn of Auber,
    In the ghoul-haunted woodland of Weir.

Here once, through an alley Titanic,
    Of cypress, I roamed with my Soul—
    Of cypress, with Psyche, my Soul.
These were days when my heart was volcanic
    As the scoriac rivers that roll—
    As the lavas that restlessly roll
Their sulphurous currents down Yaanek
    In the ultimate climes of the pole—
That groan as they roll down Mount Yaanek
    In the realms of the boreal pole.

Our talk had been serious and sober,
  But our thoughts they were palsied and sere—
  Our memories were treacherous and sere—
For we knew not the month was October,
  And we marked not the night of the year—
  (Ah, night of all nights in the year!)
We noted not the dim lake of Auber—
  (Though once we had journeyed down here),
Remembered not the dank tarn of Auber,
  Nor the ghoul-haunted woodland of Weir.


And now, as the night was senescent,
  And star-dials pointed to morn—
  As the star-dials hinted of morn—
At the end of our path a liquescent
  And nebulous lustre was born,
Out of which a miraculous crescent
  Arose with a duplicate horn—
Astarte's bediamonded crescent
  Distinct with its duplicate horn.


And I said—"She is warmer than Dian:
  She rolls through an ether of sighs—
  She revels in a region of sighs:
She has seen that the tears are not dry on
  These cheeks, where the worm never dies,
And has come past the stars of the Lion,
  To point us the path to the skies—
  To the Lethean peace of the skies—
Come up, in despite of the Lion,
  To shine on us with her bright eyes—
Come up through the lair of the Lion,
  With love in her luminous eyes."

But Psyche, uplifting her finger,
    Said—"Sadly this star I mistrust—
    Her pallor I strangely mistrust:—
Oh, hasten!—oh, let us not linger!
    Oh, fly!—let us fly!—for we must."
In terror she spoke, letting sink her
    Wings until they trailed in the dust—
In agony sobbed, letting sink her
    Plumes till they trailed in the dust—
    Till they sorrowfully trailed in the dust.


I replied—"This is nothing but dreaming:
    Let us on by this tremulous light!
    Let us bathe in this crystalline light!
Its Sybilic splendour is beaming
    With Hope and in Beauty to-night:—
    See!—it flickers up the sky through the night!
Ah, we safely may trust to its gleaming,
    And be sure it will lead us aright—
We safely may trust to a gleaming
    That cannot but guide us aright,
    Since it flickers up to Heaven through the night."


Thus I pacified Psyche and kissed her,
    And tempted her out of her gloom—
    And conquered her scruples and gloom;
And we passed to the end of the vista,
    But were stopped by the door of a tomb—
    By the door of a legended tomb;
And I said—"What is written, sweet sister,
    On the door of this legended tomb?"
    She replied—"Ulalume—Ulalume—
    'Tis the vault of thy lost Ulalume!"

Then my heart it grew ashen and sober
   As the leaves that were crisped and sere—
   As the leaves that were withering and sere—
And I cried—"It was surely October
   On *this* very night of last year
   That I journeyed—I journeyed down here—
   That I brought a dread burden down here—
   On this night of all nights in the year,
   Ah, what demon has tempted me here?
Well I know, now, this dim lake of Auber—
   This misty mid region of Weir—
Well I know, now, this dank tarn of Auber,
   This ghoul-haunted woodland of Weir."

## To Science

Science! true daughter of Old Time thou art!
  Who alterest all things with thy peering eyes.
Why preyest thou thus upon the poet's heart,
  Vulture, whose wings are dull realities?
How should he love thee? or how deem thee wise,
  Who wouldst not leave him in his wandering
To seek for treasure in the jewelled skies,
  Albeit he soared with an undaunted wing?
Hast thou not dragged Diana from her car?
  And driven the Hamadryad from the wood
To seek a shelter in some happier star?
  Hast thou not torn the Naiad from her flood,
The Elfin from the green grass, and from me
The summer dream beneath the tamarind tree?

# For Annie

Thank Heaven! the crisis—
    The danger is past,
And the lingering illness
    Is over at last—
And the fever called "Living"
    Is conquered at last.

Sadly, I know
    I am shorn of my strength,
And no muscle I move
    As I lie at full length—
But no matter!—I feel
    I am better at length.

And I rest so composedly,
    Now, in my bed,
That any beholder
    Might fancy me dead—
Might start at beholding me,
    Thinking me dead.

The moaning and groaning,
    The sighing and sobbing,
Are quieted now,
    With that horrible throbbing
At heart:—ah, that horrible,
    Horrible throbbing!

The sickness—the nausea—
    The pitiless pain—
Have ceased, with the fever
    That maddened my brain—

With the fever called "Living"
    That burned in my brain.


And oh! of all tortures
    *That* torture the worst
Has abated—the terrible
    Torture of thirst
For the naphthaline river
    Of Passion accurst:—
I have drunk of a water
    That quenches all thirst:—


Of a water that flows,
    With a lullaby sound,
From a spring but a very few
    Feet under ground—
From a cavern not very far
    Down under ground.


And ah! let it never
    Be foolishly said
That my room it is gloomy
    And narrow my bed;
For man never slept
    In a different bed—
And, *to sleep*, you must slumber
    In just such a bed.


My tantalized spirit
    Here blandly reposes.
Forgetting, or never
    Regretting its roses—
Its old agitations
    Of myrtles and roses;

For now, while so quietly
   Lying, it fancies
A holier odor
   About it, of pansies—
A rosemary odor,
   Commingled with pansies—
With rue and the beautiful
   Puritan pansies.

And so it lies happily,
   Bathing in many
A dream of the truth
   And the beauty of Annie—
Drowned in a bath
   Of the tresses of Annie.

She tenderly kissed me,
   She fondly caressed,
And then I fell gently
   To sleep on her breast—
Deeply to sleep
   From the heaven of her breast.

When the light was extinguished
   She covered me warm,
And she prayed to the angels
   To keep me from harm—
To the queen of the angels
   To shield me from harm.

And I lie so composedly,
   Now, in my bed,
(Knowing her love)
   That you fancy me dead—
And I rest so contentedly,
   Now, in my bed,

(With her love at my breast)
        That you fancy me dead—
That you shudder to look at me,
        Thinking me dead.—

But my heart it is brighter
        Than all of the many
Stars in the sky,
        For it sparkles with Annie—
It glows with the light
        Of the love of my Annie—
With the thought of the light
        Of the eyes of my Annie.

## Eldorado

        Gaily bedight,
        A gallant knight,
In sunshine and in shadow,
        Had journeyed long,
        Singing a song,
In search of Eldorado.

        But he grew old—
        This knight so bold—
And o'er his heart a shadow
        Fell as he found
        No spot of ground
That looked like Eldorado.

        And, as his strength
        Failed him at length,
He met a pilgrim shadow—
        "Shadow," said he,
        "Where can it be—
This land of Eldorado?"

> "Over the Mountains
> Of the Moon,
> Down the Valley of the Shadow,
> Ride, boldly ride,"
> The shade replied—
> "If you seek for Eldorado!"

## Dream-Land

By a route obscure and lonely,
Haunted by ill angels only,
Where an Eidolon, named NIGHT,
On a black throne reigns upright,
I have reached these lands but newly
From an ultimate dim Thule—
From a wild weird clime that lieth, sublime,
    Out of SPACE—out of TIME.

Bottomless vales and boundless floods,
And chasms, and caves, and Titan woods,
With forms that no man can discover
For the tears that drip all over;
Mountains toppling evermore
Into seas without a shore;
Seas that restlessly aspire,
Surging, unto skies of fire;
Lakes that endlessly outspread
Their lone waters—lone and dead,—
Their still waters—still and chilly
With the snows of the lolling lily.

By the lakes that thus outspread
Their lone waters, lone and dead,—
Their sad waters, sad and chilly
With the snows of the lolling lily,—
By the mountains—near the river

Murmuring lowly, murmuring ever,—
By the grey woods,—by the swamp
Where the toad and the newt encamp,—
By the dismal tarns and pools
　　Where dwell the Ghouls,—
By each spot the most unholy—
In each nook most melancholy,—
There the traveller meets, aghast,
Sheeted Memories of the Past—
Shrouded forms that start and sigh
As they pass the wanderer by—
White-robed forms of friends long given,
In agony, to the Earth—and Heaven.

For the heart whose woes are legion
'Tis a peaceful, soothing region—
For the spirit that walks in shadow
'Tis—oh 'tis an Eldorado!
But the traveller, travelling through it,
May not—dare not openly view it;
Never its mysteries are exposed
To the weak human eye unclosed;
So wills its King, who hath forbid
The uplifting of the fringèd lid;
And thus the sad Soul that here passes
Beholds it but through darkened glasses.

By a route obscure and lonely,
Haunted by ill angels only,
Where an Eidolon, named NIGHT,
On a black throne reigns upright,
I have wandered home but newly
From this ultimate dim Thule.

## *Alone*[1]

From childhood's hour I have not been
As others were—I have not seen
As others saw—I could not bring
My passions from a common spring—
From the same source I have not taken
My sorrow—I could not awaken
My heart to joy at the same tone—
And all I loved—I loved alone—
Then—in my childhood—in the dawn
Of a most stormy life—was drawn
From every depth of good and ill
The mystery which binds me still—
From the torrent, or the fountain—
From the red cliff of the mountain—
From the sun that round me roll'd
In its autumn tint of gold—
From the lightning in the sky
As it passed me flying by—
From the thunder and the storm—
And the cloud that took the form
(When the rest of Heaven was blue)
Of a demon in my view.

[1] There has always been some doubt about the authenticity of this poem. But most authorities agree with the late Professor Killis Campbell who argued that "The case for Poe's authorship . . . seems to be strong." And Philip Van Doren Stern, in *The Portable Poe*, adds that " 'Alone' is more 'Poesque' than many of his acknowledged verses."

OLIVER WENDELL HOLMES.                1809–1894

## The Last Leaf

I saw him once before,
As he passed by the door,
    And again
The pavement stones resound,
As he totters o'er the ground
    With his cane.

They say that in his prime,
Ere the pruning-knife of Time
    Cut him down,
Not a better man was found
By the Crier on his round
    Through the town.

But now he walks the streets,
And he looks at all he meets
    Sad and wan,
And he shakes his feeble head,
That it seems as if he said,
    "They are gone."

The mossy marbles rest
On the lips that he has prest
    In their bloom,
And the names he loved to hear
Have been carved for many a year
    On the tomb.

My grandmamma has said—
Poor old lady, she is dead
    Long ago—

That he had a Roman nose,
And his cheek was like a rose
   In the snow.

But now his nose is thin,
And it rests upon his chin
   Like a staff,
And a crook is in his back,
And a melancholy crack
   In his laugh.

I know it is a sin
For me to sit and grin
   At him here;
But the old three-cornered hat,
And the breeches, and all that,
   Are so queer!

And if I should live to be
The last leaf upon the tree
   In the spring,
Let them smile, as I do now,
At the old forsaken bough
   Where I cling.

### The Chambered Nautilus

This is the ship of pearl, which, poets feign,
   Sails the unshadowed main,—
     The venturous bark that flings
On the sweet summer wind its purpled wings
In gulfs enchanted, where the Siren sings,
   And coral reefs lie bare,
Where the cold sea-maids rise to sun their streaming hair.

Its webs of living gauze no more unfurl;
    Wrecked is the ship of pearl!
    And every chambered cell,
Where its dim dreaming life was wont to dwell,
As the frail tenant shaped his growing shell,
    Before thee lies revealed,—
Its irised ceiling rent, its sunless crypt unsealed!

Year after year beheld the silent toil
    That spread his lustrous coil;
    Still, as the spiral grew,
He left the past year's dwelling for the new,
Stole with soft step its shining archway through,
    Built up its idle door,
Stretched in his last-found home, and knew the old no more.

Thanks for the heavenly message brought by thee,
    Child of the wandering sea,
    Cast from her lap, forlorn!
From thy dead lips a clearer note is born
Than ever Triton blew from wreathed horn!
    While on mine ear it rings,
Through the deep caves of thought I hear a voice that
    sings,—

Build thee more stately mansions, O my soul,
    As the swift seasons roll!
    Leave thy low-vaulted past!
Let each new temple, nobler than the last,
Shut thee from heaven with a dome more vast,
    Till thou at length art free,
Leaving thine outgrown shell by life's unresting sea!

## Dorothy Q.

### A FAMILY PORTRAIT

Grandmother's mother: her age, I guess,
Thirteen summers, or something less;
Girlish bust, but womanly air;
Smooth, square forehead with uprolled hair;
Lips that lover has never kissed;
Taper fingers and slender wrist;
Hanging sleeves of stiff brocade;
So they painted the little maid.

On her hand a parrot green
Sits unmoving and broods serene.
Hold up the canvas full in view,—
Look! there's a rent the light shines through,
Dark with a century's fringe of dust,—
That was a Red-Coat's rapier-thrust!
Such is the tale the lady old,
Dorothy's daughter's daughter, told.

Who the painter was none may tell,—
One whose best was not over well;
Hard and dry, it must be confessed,
Flat as a rose that has long been pressed;
Yet in her cheek the hues are bright,
Dainty colors of red and white,
And in her slender shape are seen
Hint and promise of stately mien.

Look not on her with eyes of scorn,—
Dorothy Q. was a lady born!
Ay! since the galloping Normans came,
England's annals have known her name;

And still to the three-hilled rebel town
Dear is that ancient name's renown,
For many a civic wreath they won,
The youthful sire and the gray-haired son.

O Damsel Dorothy! Dorothy Q.!
Strange is the gift that I owe to you;
Such a gift as never a king
Save to daughter or son might bring,—
All my tenure of heart and hand,
All my title to house and land;
Mother and sister and child and wife
And joy and sorrow and death and life!

What if a hundred years ago
Those close-shut lips had answered No,
When forth the tremulous question came
That cost the maiden her Norman name,
And under the folds that look so still
The bodice swelled with the bosom's thrill?
Should I be I, or would it be
One tenth another, to nine tenths me?

Soft is the breath of a maiden's YES:
Not the light gossamer stirs with less;
But never a cable that holds so fast
Through all the battles of wave and blast,
And never an echo of speech or song
That lives in the babbling air so long!
There were tones in the voice that whispered then
You may hear to-day in a hundred men.

O lady and lover, how faint and far
Your images hover,—and here we are
Solid and stirring in flesh and bone,—
Edward's and Dorothy's—all their own,—

A goodly record for Time to show
Of a syllable spoken so long ago!—
Shall I bless you, Dorothy, or forgive
For the tender whisper that bade me live?

It shall be a blessing, my little maid!
I will heal the stab of the Red-Coat's blade,
And freshen the gold of the tarnished frame,
And gild with a rhyme your household name;
So you shall smile on us brave and bright
As first you greeted the morning's light,
And live untroubled by woes and fears
Through a second youth of a hundred years.

JONES VERY                                    1813–1880

## The Spirit-Land

Father! thy wonders do not singly stand,
Nor far removed where feet have seldom strayed;
Around us ever lies the enchanted land,
In marvels rich to thine own sons displayed.
In finding thee are all things round us found;
In losing thee are all things lost beside;
Ears have we, but in vain strange voices sound;
And to our eyes the vision is denied.
We wander in the country far remote,
Mid tombs and ruined piles in death to dwell;
Or on the records of past greatness dote,
And for a buried soul the living sell;
While on our path bewildered falls the night
That ne'er returns us to the fields of light.

### The Latter Rain

The latter rain,—it falls in anxious haste
Upon the sun-dried fields and branches bare,
Loosening with searching drops the rigid waste
As if it would each root's lost strength repair;
But not a blade grows green as in the spring;
No swelling twig puts forth its thickening leaves;
The robins only mid the harvests sing,
Pecking the grain that scatters from the sheaves;
The rain falls still,—the fruit all ripened drops,
It pierces chestnut-burr and walnut-shell;
The furrowed fields disclose the yellow crops;
Each bursting pod of talents used can tell;
And all that once received the early rain
Declare to man it was not sent in vain.

### Nature

The bubbling brook doth leap when I come by,
Because my feet find measure with its call;
The birds know when the friend they love is nigh,
For I am known to them, both great and small.
The flower that on the lonely hill-side grows
Expects me there when Spring its bloom has given;
And many a tree and bush my wanderings knows,
And e'en the clouds and silent stars of heaven;
For he who with his Maker walks aright,
Shall be their lord as ADAM was before;
His ear shall catch each sound with new delight,
Each object wear the dress that then it wore;
And he, as when erect in soul he stood,
Hear from his Father's lips that all is good.

JOHN GODFREY SAXE                        1816–1887

## Early Rising

"God bless the man who first invented sleep!"
   So Sancho Panza said, and so say I:
And bless him, also, that he didn't keep
   His great discovery to himself; nor try
To make it—as the lucky fellow might—
A close monopoly by patent-right!

Yes—bless the man who first invented sleep,
   (I really can't avoid the iteration;)
But blast the man, with curses loud and deep,
   Whate'er the rascal's name, or age, or station,
Who first invented, and went round advising,
That artificial cut-off—Early Rising!

"Rise with the lark, and with the lark to bed,"
   Observes some solemn, sentimental owl;
Maxims like these are very cheaply said;
   But, ere you make yourself a fool or fowl,
Pray just inquire about his rise and fall,
And whether larks have any beds at all!

The time for honest folks to be a-bed
   Is in the morning, if I reason right;
And he who cannot keep his precious head
   Upon his pillow till it's fairly light,
And so enjoy his forty morning winks,
Is up to knavery; or else—he drinks!

Thompson, who sung about the "Seasons," said
 It was a glorious thing to *rise* in season;
But then he said it—lying—in his bed,
 At ten o'clock A.M.,—the very reason
He wrote so charmingly. The simple fact is
His preaching wasn't sanctioned by his practice.

'Tis, doubtless, well to be sometimes awake,—
 Awake to duty, and awake to truth,—
But when, alas! a nice review we take
 Of our best deeds and days, we find, in sooth,
The hours that leave the slightest cause to weep
Are those we passed in childhood or asleep!

'Tis beautiful to leave the world awhile
 For the soft visions of the gentle night;
And free, at last, from mortal care or guile,
 To live as only in the angel's sight,
In sleep's sweet realm so cosily shut in,
Where, at the worst, we only *dream* of sin!

So let us sleep, and give the Maker praise.
 I like the lad who, when his father thought
To clip his morning nap by hackneyed phrase
 Of vagrant worm by early songster caught,
Cried, "Served him right!—it's not at all surprising;
The worm was punished, sir, for early rising!"

# HENRY DAVID THOREAU                    1817–1862

## Mist

Low-anchored cloud,
Newfoundland air,
Fountain-head and source of rivers,
Dew-cloth, dream-drapery,
And napkin spread by fays;
Drifting meadow of the air,
Where bloom the daisied banks and violets,
And in whose fenny labyrinth
The bittern booms and heron wades;
Spirit of lakes and seas and rivers,—
Bear only perfumes and the scent
Of healing herbs to just men's fields.

## Smoke

Light-wingèd Smoke! Icarian bird,
Melting thy pinions in thy upward flight;
Lark without song, and messenger of dawn,
Circling above the hamlets as thy nest;
Or else, departing dream, and shadowy form
Of midnight vision, gathering up thy skirts;
By night star-veiling, and by day
Darkening the light and blotting out the sun;
Go thou, my incense, upward from this hearth,
And ask the gods to pardon this clear flame.

## Independence

My life more civil is and free
Than any civil polity.

Ye princes, keep your realms
  And circumscribéd power,
Not wide as are my dreams,
  Nor rich as is this hour.

What can ye give which I have not?
What can ye take which I have got?
  Can ye defend the dangerless?
  Can ye inherit nakedness?

To all true wants Time's ear is deaf,
Penurious States lend no relief
    Out of their pelf:
  But a free soul—thank God—
    Can help itself.

    Be sure your fate
Doth keep apart its state,—
Not linked with any band,
Even the noblest in the land,—

In tented fields with cloth of gold
  No place doth hold,
But is more chivalrous than they are,
  And sigheth for a nobler war;

A finer strain its trumpet rings,
A brighter gleam its armor flings.

The life that I aspire to live,
  No man proposeth me;
No trade upon the street
  Wears its emblazonry.

# JAMES RUSSELL LOWELL                    1819–1891

## *Lincoln*

FROM THE "COMMEMORATION ODE"

Life may be given in many ways,
    And loyalty to Truth be sealed
As bravely in the closet as the field,
        So bountiful is Fate;
        But then to stand beside her,
        When craven churls deride her,
To front a lie in arms and not to yield,
        This shows, methinks, God's plan
        And measure of a stalwart man,
        Limbed like the old heroic breeds,
        Who stand self-poised on manhood's solid earth,
    Not forced to frame excuses for his birth,
Fed from within with all the strength he needs.

Such was he, our Martyr-Chief,
    Whom late the Nation he had led,
    With ashes on her head,
Wept with the passion of an angry grief:
Forgive me, if from present things I turn
To speak what in my heart will beat and burn,
And hang my wreath on his world-honored urn.
        Nature, they say, doth dote,
        And cannot make a man
        Save on some worn-out plan,
        Repeating us by rote:
For him her Old-World moulds aside he threw,
    And, choosing sweet clay from the breast
        Of the unexhausted West,

With stuff untainted shaped a hero new,
Wise, steadfast in the strength of God, and true.
    How beautiful to see
Once more a shepherd of mankind indeed,
Who loved his charge, but never loved to lead;
One whose meek flock the people joyed to be,
    Not lured by any cheat of birth,
    But by his clear-grained human worth,
And brave old wisdom of sincerity!
    They knew that outward grace is dust;
    They could not choose but trust
In that sure-footed mind's unfaltering skill,
    And supple-tempered will
That bent like perfect steel to spring again and thrust.
  His was no lonely mountain-peak of mind,
  Thrusting to thin air o'er our cloudy bars,
  A sea-mark now, now lost in vapors blind;
  Broad prairie rather, genial, level-lined,
  Fruitful and friendly for all human kind,
Yet also nigh to heaven and loved of loftiest stars.
    Nothing of Europe here,
Or, then, of Europe fronting mornward still,
    Ere any names of Serf and Peer
  Could Nature's equal scheme deface;
  Here was a type of the true elder race,
And one of Plutarch's men talked with us face to face.
  I praise him not; it were too late;
And some innative weakness there must be
In him who condescends to victory
Such as the Present gives, and cannot wait,
    Safe in himself as in a fate.
    So always firmly he:
    He knew to bide his time,
    And can his fame abide,
Still patient in his simple faith sublime,
    Till the wise years decide.

Great captains, with their guns and drums,
　　Disturb our judgment for the hour,
　　　But at last silence comes;
These all are gone, and, standing like a tower,
Our children shall behold his fame,
　　The kindly-earnest, brave, foreseeing man,
Sagacious, patient, dreading praise, not blame,
New birth of our new soil, the first American.

## Auspex

My heart, I cannot still it,
Nest that had song-birds in it;
And when the last shall go,
The dreary days, to fill it,
Instead of lark or linnet,
Shall whirl dead leaves and snow.

Had they been swallows only,
Without the passion stronger
That skyward longs and sings,—
Woe's me, I shall be lonely
When I can feel no longer
The impatience of their wings!

A moment, sweet delusion,
Like birds the brown leaves hover;
But it will not be long
Before their wild confusion
Fall wavering down to cover
The poet and his song.

### Aladdin

When I was a beggarly boy,
    And lived in a cellar damp,
I had not a friend nor a toy,
    But I had Aladdin's lamp;
When I could not sleep for cold,
    I had fire enough in my brain,
And builded, with roofs of gold,
    My beautiful castles in Spain!

Since then I have toiled day and night,
    I have money and power good store,
But I'd give all my lamps of silver bright,
    For the one that is mine no more;
Take, Fortune, whatever you choose,
    You gave, and may snatch again;
I have nothing 't would pain me to lose,
    For I own no more castles in Spain!

### June

FROM "THE VISION OF SIR LAUNFAL"

Earth gets its price for what Earth gives us;
    The beggar is taxed for a corner to die in,
The priest hath his fee who comes and shrives us,
    We bargain for the graves we lie in;
At the Devil's booth are all things sold,
Each ounce of dross costs its ounce of gold;
    For a cap and bells our lives we pay,
Bubbles we earn with a whole soul's tasking:
    'T is heaven alone that is given away,
'T is only God may be had for the asking;
No price is set on the lavish summer,
And June may be had by the poorest comer.

And what is so rare as a day in June?
    Then, if ever, come perfect days;
Then Heaven tries the earth if it be in tune,
    And over it softly her warm ear lays:
Whether we look, or whether we listen,
We hear life murmur, or see it glisten;
Every clod feels a stir of might,
    An instinct within it that reaches and towers
And, groping blindly above it for light,
    Climbs to a soul in grass and flowers;
The flush of life may well be seen
    Thrilling back over hills and valleys;
The cowslip startles in meadows green,
    The buttercup catches the sun in its chalice
And there 's never a leaf or a blade too mean
    To be some happy creature's palace;
The little bird sits at his door in the sun,
    Atilt like a blossom among the leaves,
And lets his illumined being o'errun
    With the deluge of summer it receives;
His mate feels the eggs beneath her wings,
And the heart in her dumb breast flutters and sings;
He sings to the wide world, and she to her nest,—
In the nice ear of Nature, which song is the best?

Now is the high-tide of the year,
    And whatever of life hath ebbed away
Comes flooding back, with a ripply cheer,
    Into every bare inlet and creek and bay;
Now the heart is so full that a drop overfills it,
We are happy now because God wills it;
No matter how barren the past may have been,
'T is enough for us now that the leaves are green;
We sit in the warm shade and feel right well
How the sap creeps up and the blossoms swell;

We may shut our eyes, but we cannot help knowing
That skies are clear and grass is growing;
The breeze comes whispering in our ear,
That dandelions are blossoming near,
    That maize has sprouted, that streams are flowing,
That the river is bluer than the sky,
That the robin is plastering his house hard by;
And if the breeze kept the good news back,
For other couriers we should not lack;
    We could guess it all by yon heifer's lowing,—
And hark! how clear bold chanticleer,
Warmed with the new wine of the year,
    Tells all in his lusty crowing!


Joy comes, grief goes, we know not how;
Everything is happy now,
    Everything is upward striving;
'T is as easy now for the heart to be true
As for grass to be green or skies to be blue,—
    'T is the natural way of living:
Who knows whither the clouds have fled?
    In the unscarred heaven they leave no wake,
And the eyes forget the tears they have shed,
    The heart forgets its sorrow and ache;
The soul partakes the season's youth,
    And the sulphurous rifts of passion and woe
Lie deep 'neath a silence pure and smooth,
    Like burnt-out craters healed with snow.


### To Henry Wadsworth Longfellow

I need not praise the sweetness of his song,
    Where limpid verse to limpid verse succeeds
Smooth as our Charles, when, fearing lest he wrong
The new moon's mirrored skiff, he slides along,
    Full without noise, and whispers in his reeds.

With loving breath of all the winds his name
  Is blown about the world, but to his friends
A sweeter secret hides behind his fame,
And Love steals shyly through the loud acclaim
  To murmur a *God bless you!* and there ends.

As I muse backward up the checkered years,
  Wherein so much was given, so much was lost,
Blessings in both kinds, such as cheapen tears—
But hush! this is not for profaner ears;
  Let them drink molten pearls nor dream the cost.

Some suck up poison from a sorrow's core,
  As naught but nightshade grew upon earth's ground;
Love turned all his to heart's-ease, and the more
Fate tried his bastions, she but forced a door,
  Leading to sweeter manhood and more sound.

Even as a wind-waved fountain's swaying shade
  Seems of mixed race, a gray wraith shot with sun,
So through his trial faith translucent rayed,
Till darkness, half disnatured so, betrayed
  A heart of sunshine that would fain o'errun.

Surely if skill in song the shears may stay,
  And of its purpose cheat the charmed abyss,
If our poor life be lengthened by a lay,
He shall not go, although his presence may,
  And the next age in praise shall double this.

Long days be his, and each as lusty-sweet
  As gracious natures find his song to be;
May Age steal on with softly cadenced feet
Falling in music, as for him were meet
  Whose choicest verse is harsher-toned than he!

## Yussouf

A stranger came one night to Yussouf's tent,
Saying, "Behold one outcast and in dread,
Against whose life the bow of power is bent,
Who flies, and hath not where to lay his head;
I come to thee for shelter and for food,
To Yussouf, called through all our tribes 'The Good.'"

"This tent is mine," said Yussouf, "but no more
Than it is God's; come in, and be at peace;
Freely shalt thou partake of all my store
As I of his who buildeth over these
Our tents his glorious roof of night and day,
And at whose door none ever yet heard Nay."

So Yussouf entertained his guest that night,
And, waking him ere day, said: "Here is gold,
My swiftest horse is saddled for thy flight,
Depart before the prying day grow bold."
As one lamp lights another, nor grows less,
So nobleness enkindleth nobleness.

That inward light the stranger's face made grand,
Which shines from all self-conquest; kneeling low,
He bowed his forehead upon Yussouf's hand,
Sobbing: "O Sheik, I cannot leave thee so;
I will repay thee; all this thou hast done
Unto that Ibrahim who slew thy son!"

"Take thrice the gold," said Yussouf, "for with thee
Into the desert, never to return,
My one black thought shall ride away from me;
First-born, for whom by day and night I yearn,
Balanced and just are all of God's decrees;
Thou art avenged, my first-born, sleep in peace!"

## What Mr. Robinson Thinks

Guvener B. is a sensible man;
   He stays to his home an' looks arter his folks;
He draws his furrer ez straight ez he can,
   An' into nobody's tater-patch pokes;
        But John P.
        Robinson he
   Sez he wunt vote fer Guvener B.

My! aint it terrible? Wut shall we du?
   We can't never choose him o' course,—thet's flat;
Guess we shall hev to come round (don't you?)
   An' go in fer thunder an' guns, an' all that;
        Fer John P.
        Robinson he
   Sez he wunt vote fer Guvener B.

Gineral C. is a dreffle smart man:
   He's ben on all sides thet give places or pelf;
But consistency still wuz a part of his plan,—
   He's been true to *one* party,—an' thet is himself;—
        So John P.
        Robinson he
   Sez he shall vote fer Gineral C.

Gineral C. he goes in fer the war;
   He don't vally princerple more'n an old cud;
Wut did God make us raytional creeturs fer,
   But glory an' gunpowder, plunder an' blood?
        So John P.
        Robinson he
   Sez he shall vote fer Gineral C.

We were gittin' on nicely up here to our village,
   With good old idees o' wut's right an' wut aint,

We kind o' thought Christ went agin war an' pillage,
   An' thet eppyletts worn't the best mark of a saint;
           But John P.
           Robinson he
   Sez this kind o' thing's an exploded idee.

The side of our country must ollers be took,
   An' President Polk, you know, *he* is our country,
An' the angel thet writes all our sins in a book
   Puts the *debit* to him, an' to us the *per contry*
           An' John P.
           Robinson he
   Sez this is his view o' the thing to a T.

Parson Wilbur he calls all these argimunts lies;
   Sez they're nothin' on airth but jest *fee, faw, fum;*
An' thet all this big talk of our destinies
   Is half on it ign'ance, an' t'other half rum;
           But John P.
           Robinson he
   Sez it aint no sech thing; an', of course, so must we.

Parson Wilbur sez *he* never heerd in his life
   Thet th' Apostles rigged out in their swaller-tail coats,
An' marched round in front of a drum an' a fife,
   To git some on 'em office, an' some on 'em votes;
           But John P.
           Robinson he
   Sez they didn't know everythin' down in Judee.

Wal, it's a marcy we've gut folks to tell us
   The rights an' the wrongs o' these matters, I vow,—
God sends country lawyers, an' other wise fellers,
   To start the world's team wen it gits in a slough;
           Fer John P.
           Robinson he
   Sez the world'll go right, ef he hollers out Gee!

## Freedom

Men! whose boast it is that ye
Come of fathers brave and free,
If there breathe on earth a slave,
Are ye truly free and brave?
If ye do not feel the chain,
When it works a brother's pain,
Are ye not base slaves indeed,
Slaves unworthy to be freed?

Women! who shall one day bear
Sons to breathe New England air.
If ye hear, without a blush,
Deeds to make the roused blood **rush**
Like red lava through your veins,
For your sisters now in chains,—
Answer! are ye fit to be
Mothers of the brave and free?

Is true Freedom but to break
Fetters for our own dear sake,
And, with leathern hearts, forget
That we owe mankind a debt?
No! true freedom is to share
All the chains our brothers wear,
And, with heart and hand, to be
Earnest to make others free!

They are slaves who fear to speak
For the fallen and the weak;
They are slaves who will not choose
Hatred, scoffing, and abuse,
Rather than in silence shrink,
From the truth they needs must think;
They are slaves who dare not be
In the right with two or three.

## In Absence

These rugged, wintry days I scarce could bear,
Did I not know, that, in the early spring,
When wild March winds upon their errands sing,
Thou wouldst return, bursting on this still air,
Like those same winds, when, startled from their lair,
They hunt up violets, and free swift brooks
From icy cares, even as thy clear looks
Bid my heart bloom, and sing, and break all care:
When drops with welcome rain the April day,
My flowers shall find their April in thine eyes,
Save there the rain in dreary clouds doth stay,
As loath to fall out of those happy skies;
Yet sure, my love, thou art most like to May,
That comes with steady sun when April dies.

## The Fountain

Into the sunshine,
    Full of the light,
Leaping and flashing
    From morn till night!

Into the moonlight,
    Whiter than snow,
Waving so flower-like
    When the winds blow!

Into the starlight
    Rushing in spray,
Happy at midnight,
    Happy by day!

Ever in motion,
  Blithesome and cheery,
Still climbing heavenward,
  Never aweary;—

Glad of all weathers,
  Still seeming best,
Upward or downward,
  Motion thy rest;—

Full of a nature
  Nothing can tame,
Changed every moment,
  Ever the same;—

Ceaseless aspiring,
  Ceaseless content,
Darkness or sunshine
  Thy element;—

Glorious fountain!
  Let my heart be
Fresh, changeful, constant,
  Upward, like thee!

# JULIA WARD HOWE
1819–1910

## Battle-Hymn of the Republic

Mine eyes have seen the glory of the coming of the Lord:
He is trampling out the vintage where the grapes of wrath are
    stored;
He hath loosed the fateful lightning of His terrible swift
    sword:
  His truth is marching on.

I have seen Him in the watch-fires of a hundred circling
    camps;
They have builded Him an altar in the evening dews and
    damps;
I can read His righteous sentence by the dim and flaring
    lamps.
  His day is marching on.

I have read a fiery gospel, writ in burnished rows of steel:
"As ye deal with my contemners, so with you my grace shall
    deal;
Let the Hero, born of woman, crush the serpent with his heel,
  Since God is marching on."

He has sounded forth the trumpet that shall never call retreat;
He is sifting out the hearts of men before His judgment-seat:
Oh, be swift, my soul, to answer Him! be jubilant, my feet!
  Our God is marching on.

In the beauty of the lilies Christ was born across the sea,
With a glory in His bosom that transfigures you and me:
As He died to make men holy, let us die to make men free,
  While God is marching on.

## HERMAN MELVILLE                      1819–1891

### From *"The Martyr"*

Good Friday was the day
  Of the prodigy and crime,
When they killed him in his pity,
  When they killed him in his prime
Of clemency and calm—
    When with yearning he was filled
    To redeem the evil-willed,
And, though conqueror, be kind;
  But they killed him in his kindness,
  In their madness and their blindness,
And they killed him from behind.

  There is sobbing of the strong,
    And a pall upon the land;
  But the People in their weeping
    Bare the iron hand;
  Beware the People weeping
    When they bare the iron hand.

He lieth in his blood—
  The father in his face;
They have killed him, the Forgiver—
  The Avenger takes his place,
The Avenger wisely stern,
    Who in righteousness shall do
    What the heavens call him to,
And the parricides remand;
  For they killed him in his kindness,
  In their madness and their blindness,
And his blood is on their hand.

  There is sobbing of the strong,
    And a pall upon the land;

But the People in their weeping
Bare the iron hand;
Beware the People weeping
When they bare the iron hand.

## The Night-March

With banners furled, the clarions mute,
An army passes in the night;
And beaming spears and helms salute
The dark with bright.

In silence deep the legions stream,
With open ranks, in order true;
Over boundless plains they stream and gleam—
No chief in view!

Afar, in twinkling distance lost,
(So legends tell) he lonely wends
And back through all that shining host
His mandate sends.

## L'Envoi

THE RETURN OF THE SIRE DE NESLE: A.D. 16—

My towers at last! These rovings end,
Their thirst is slaked in larger dearth:
The yearning infinite recoils,
For terrible is earth.

Kaf thrusts his snouted crags through fog:
Araxes swells beyond his span,
And knowledge poured by pilgrimage
Overflows the banks of man.

But thou, my stay, thy lasting love
One lonely good, let this but be!
Weary to view the wide world's swarm,
But blest to fold but thee.

# WALT WHITMAN                                    1819–1892

## Poets to Come

Poets to come! orators, singers, musicians to come!
Not to-day is to justify me and answer what I am for,
But you, a new brood, native, athletic, continental, greater
    than before known,
Arouse! for you must justify me.

I myself but write one or two indicative words for the future,
I but advance a moment only to wheel and hurry back in the
    darkness.

I am a man who, sauntering along without fully stopping,
    turns a casual look upon you and then averts his face,
Leaving it to you to prove and define it,
Expecting the main things from you.

## I Hear America Singing

I hear America singing, the varied carols I hear,
Those of mechanics, each one singing his as it should be blithe
    and strong,
The carpenter singing his as he measures his plank or beam,
The mason singing his as he makes ready for work, or leaves
    off work,
The boatman singing what belongs to him in his boat, the
    deckhand singing on the steamboat deck,
The shoemaker singing as he sits on his bench, the hatter
    singing as he stands,
The wood-cutter's song, the plowboy's on his way in the
    morning, or at noon intermission or at sundown,
The delicious singing of the mother, or of the young wife at
    work, or of the girl sewing or washing,
Each singing what belongs to him or her and to none else,
The day what belongs to the day—at night the party of young
    fellows, robust, friendly,
Singing with open mouths their strong melodious songs.

## From *"Song of Myself"*

### 1

I celebrate myself, and sing myself,
And what I assume you shall assume,
For every atom belonging to me as good belongs to you.

I loafe and invite my soul,
I learn and loafe at my ease observing a spear of summer
    grass.

My tongue, every atom of my blood, form'd from this soil,
    this air,
Born here of parents born here from parents the same, and
    their parents the same,
I, now thirty-seven years old in perfect health begin,
Hoping to cease not till death.
Creeds and schools in abeyance,
Retiring back a while suffic'd at what they are, but never for-
    gotten,
I harbor for good or bad, I permit to speak at every hazard,
Nature without check with original energy.

### 3

I have heard what the talkers were talking, the talk of the
    beginning and the end,
But I do not talk of the beginning or the end.

There was never any more inception than there is now,
Nor any more youth or age than there is now,
And will never be any more perfection than there is now,
Nor any more heaven or hell than there is now.

Urge and urge and urge,
Always the procreant urge of the world.

Out of the dimness opposite equals advance, always sub-
    stance and increase, always sex,
Always a knit of identity, always distinction, always a breed
    of life.


To elaborate is no avail, learn'd and unlearn'd feel that it is so.


Sure as the most certain sure, plumb in the uprights, well
    center-tied, braced in the beams,
Stout as a horse, affectionate, haughty, electrical,
I and this mystery here we stand.
Clear and sweet is my soul, and clear and sweet is all that is
    not my soul.


Lack one lacks both, and the unseen is proved by the seen,
Till that becomes unseen and receives proof in its turn.


6

A child said, *What is the grass?* fetching it to me with full
    hands;
How could I answer the child? I do not know what it is any
    more than he.


I guess it must be the flag of my disposition, out of hopeful
    green stuff woven.
Or I guess it is the handkerchief of the Lord,
A scented gift and remembrancer designedly dropt,
Bearing the owner's name someway in the corner, that we
    may see and remark, and say *Whose?*


Or I guess the grass is itself a child, the produced babe of the
    vegetation.
Or I guess it is a uniform hieroglyphic,
And it means, Sprouting alike in broad zones and narrow
    zones,

Growing among black folks as among white,
Kanuck, Tuckahoe, Congressman, Cuff, I give them the same,
     I receive them the same.

And now it seems to me the beautiful uncut hair of graves.

Tenderly will I use you curling grass,
It may be you transpire from the breasts of young men,
It may be if I had known them I would have loved them,
It may be you are from old people, or from offspring taken
     soon out of their mothers' laps,
And here you are the mothers' laps.

This grass is very dark to be from the white heads of old
     mothers,
Darker than the colorless beards of old men,
Dark to come from under the faint red roofs of mouths.
O I perceive after all so many uttering tongues,
And I perceive they do not come from the roofs of mouths
     for nothing.
I wish I could translate the hints about the dead young men
     and women,
And the hints about old men and mothers, and the offspring
     taken soon out of their laps.

What do you think has become of the young and old men?
And what do you think has become of the women and chil-
     dren?

They are alive and well somewhere,
The smallest sprout shows there is really no death,
And if ever there was it led forward life, and does not wait
     at the end to arrest it,
And ceas'd the moment life appear'd.

All goes onward and outward, nothing collapses,
And to die is different from what anyone supposed, and
    luckier.

### 7

Has anyone supposed it lucky to be born?
I hasten to inform him or her it is just as lucky to die, and I
    know it.

I pass death with the dying and birth with the new-wash'd
    babe, and am not contain'd between my hat and boots,
And peruse manifold objects, no two alike and every one
    good,
The earth good and the stars good, and their adjuncts all
    good.
I am not an earth nor an adjunct of an earth,
I am the mate and companion of people, all just as immortal
    and fathomless as myself,
(They do not know how immortal, but I know.)

### 8

The little one sleeps in its cradle,
I lift the gauze and look a long time, and silently brush away
    flies with my hand.

The youngster and the red-faced girl turn aside up the bushy
    hill,
I peeringly view them from the top.

The suicide sprawls on the bloody floor of the bedroom,
I witness the corpse with its dabbled hair, I note where the
    pistol has fallen.

The blab of the pave, tires of carts, sluff of boot-soles, talk of
    the promenaders,

The heavy omnibus, the driver with his interrogating thumb,
    the clank of the shod horses on the granite floor,
The snow-sleighs, clinking, shouted jokes, pelts of snow-balls,
The hurrahs for popular favorites, the fury of rous'd mobs,
The flap of the curtain'd litter, a sick man inside borne to the
    hospital,
The meeting of enemies, the sudden oath, the blows and fall,
The excited crowd, the policeman with his star quickly work-
    ing his passage to the centre of the crowd,
The impassive stones that receive and return so many echoes,
What groans of over-fed or half-starv'd who fall sunstruck or
    in fits,
What exclamations of women taken suddenly who hurry home
    and give birth to babes,
What living and buried speech is always vibrating here, what
    howls restrain'd by decorum,
Arrests of criminals, slights, adulterous offers made, accept-
    ances, rejections with convex lips,
I mind them or the show or resonance of them—I come and
    I depart.

9

The doors of the country barn stand open and ready,
The dried grass of the harvest-time loads the slow-drawn
    wagon,
The clear light plays on the brown gray and green intertinged,
The armfuls are pack'd to the sagging mow.

I am there, I help, I came stretch'd atop of the load,
I felt its soft jolts, one leg reclined on the other,
I jump from the cross-beams and seize the clover and timothy,
And roll head over heels and tangle my hair full of wisps.

10

Alone far in the wilds and mountains I hunt,
Wandering amazed at my own lightness and glee,
In the late afternoon choosing a safe spot to pass the night,

Kindling a fire and broiling the fresh-kill'd game,
Falling asleep on the gather'd leaves with my dog and gun by
    my side.


The Yankee clipper is under her sky-sails, she cuts the sparkle
    and scud,
My eyes settle the land, I bend at her prow or shout joyously
    from the deck.


The boatmen and clam-diggers arose early and stopt for me,
I tuck'd my trowser-ends in my boots and went and had a
    good time;
You should have been with us that day round the chowder-
    kettle.


I saw the marriage of the trapper in the open air in the far
    west, the bride was a red girl,
Her father and his friends sat near cross-legged and dumbly
    smoking, they had moccasins to their feet and large
    thick blankets hanging from their shoulders,
On a bank lounged the trapper, he was drest mostly in skins,
    his luxuriant beard and curls protected his neck, he held
    his bride by the hand,
She had long eyelashes, her head was bare, her coarse straight
    locks descended upon her voluptuous limbs and reach'd
    to her feet.


The runaway slave came to my house and stopt outside,
I heard his motions crackling the twigs of the woodpile,
Through the swung half-door of the kitchen I saw him limpsy
    and weak,
And went where he sat on a log and led him in and assured
    him,
And brought water and fill'd a tub for his sweated body and
    bruis'd feet,

And gave him a room that enter'd from my own, and gave
  him some coarse clean clothes,
And remember perfectly well his revolving eyes and his awk-
  wardness,
And remember putting plasters on the galls of his neck and
  ankles;
He staid with me a week before he was recuperated and
  pass'd north,
I had him sit next me at table, my fire-lock lean'd in the
  corner.

15

The pure contralto sings in the organ loft,
The carpenter dresses his plank, the tongue of his foreplane
  whistles its wild ascending lisp,
The married and unmarried children ride home to their
  Thanksgiving dinner,
The pilot seizes the king-pin, he heaves down with a strong
  arm,
The mate stands braced in the whale-boat, lance and harpoon
  are ready,
The duck-shooter walks by silent and cautious stretches,
The deacons are ordain'd with cross'd hands at the altar,
The spinning-girl retreats and advances to the hum of the big
  wheel,
The farmer stops by the bars as he walks on a First-day loaf
  and looks at the oats and rye,
The lunatic is carried at last to the asylum a confirm'd case,
(He will never sleep any more as he did in the cot in his
  mother's bedroom;)
The jour printer with gray head and gaunt jaws works at his
  case,
He turns his quid of tobacco while his eyes blur with the
  manuscript;
The malform'd limbs are tied to the surgeon's table,

What is removed drops horribly in a pail;

The quadroon girl is sold at the auction-stand, the drunkard
    nods by the bar-room stove,

The machinist rolls up his sleeves, the policeman travels his
    beat, the gate-keeper marks who pass,

The young fellow drives the express-wagon, (I love him,
    though I do not know him;)

The half-breed straps on his light boots to compete in the race,

The western turkey-shooting draws old and young, some lean
    on their rifles, some sit on logs,

Out from the crowd steps the marksman, takes his position,
    levels his piece;

The groups of newly-come immigrants cover the wharf or
    levee,

As the woolly-pates hoe in the sugar-field, the overseer views
    them from his saddle,

The bugle calls in the ball-room, the gentlemen run for their
    partners, the dancers bow to each other,

The youth lies awake in the cedar-roof'd garret and harks to
    the musical rain,

The Wolverine sets traps on the creek that helps fill the
    Huron,

The squaw wrapt in her yellow-hemm'd cloth is offering moc-
    casins and bead-bags for sale,

The connoisseur peers along the exhibition-gallery with half-
    shut eyes bent sideways,

As the deck-hands make fast the steamboat the plank is
    thrown for the shore-going passengers,

The young sister holds out the skein while the elder sister
    winds it off in a ball, and stops now and then for the
    knots,

The one-year wife is recovering and happy having a week ago
    borne her first child,

The clean-hair'd Yankee girl works with her sewing machine
    or in the factory or mill,

The paving-man leans on his two-handed rammer, the re-
  porter's lead flies swiftly over the note-book, the sign-
  painter is lettering with blue and gold,

The canal boy trots on the tow-path, the book-keeper counts
  at his desk, the shoe-maker waxes his thread,

The conductor beats time for the band and all the performers
  follow him,

The child is baptized, the convert is making his first profession,

The regatta is spread on the bay, the race is begun, (how the
  white sails sparkle!)

The drover watching his drove sings out to them that would
  stray,

The peddler sweats with his pack on his back, (the purchaser
  higgling about the odd cent;)

The bride unrumples her white dress, the minute-hand of the
  clock moves slowly,

The opium-eater reclines with rigid head and just-open'd lips,

The prostitute draggles her shawl, her bonnet bobs on her
  tipsy and pimpled neck,

The crowd laugh at her blackguard oaths, the men jeer and
  wink to each other,

(Miserable! I do not laugh at your oaths nor jeer you;)

The President holding a cabinet council is surrounded by the
  great Secretaries,

On the piazza walk three matrons stately and friendly with
  twined arms,

The crew of the fish-smack pack repeated layers of halibut in
  the hold,

Coon-seekers go through the regions of the Red river or
  through those drain'd by the Tennessee, or through those
  of the Arkansas,

Torches shine in the dark that hangs on the Chattahooche or
  Altamahaw,

Patriarchs sit at supper with sons and grandsons and great
 grandsons around them,
In walls of adobie, in canvas tents, rest hunters and trappers
 after their day's sport,
The city sleeps and the country sleeps,
The living sleep for their time, the dead sleep for their time,
The old husband sleeps by his wife and the young husband
 sleeps by his wife;
And these tend inward to me, and I tend outward to them,
And such as it is to be of these more or less I am,
And of these one and all I weave the song of myself.

18

With music strong I come, with my cornets and my drums,
I play not marches for accepted victors only, I play marches
 for conquer'd and slain persons.

Have you heard that it was good to gain the day?
I also say it is good to fall, battles are lost in the same spirit
 in which they are won.

I beat and pound for the dead,
I blow through my embouchures my loudest and gayest for
 them.

Vivas to those who have fail'd!
And to those whose war-vessels sank in the sea!
And to those themselves who sank in the sea!
And to all generals that lost engagements, and all overcome
 heroes!
And the numberless unknown heroes equal to the greatest
 heroes known!

### 19

This is the meal equally set, this the meat for natural hunger,
It is for the wicked just the same as the righteous, I make
    appointments with all,
I will not have a single person slighted or left away,
The kept-woman, sponger, thief, are hereby invited,
There shall be no difference between them and the rest.

This is the press of a bashful hand, this the float and odor of
    hair,
This the touch of my lips to yours, this the murmur of yearn-
    ing,
This the far-off depth and height reflecting my own face,
This the thoughtful merge of myself, and the outlet again.
Do you guess I have some intricate purpose?
Well I have, for the Fourth-month showers have, and the
    mica on the side of the rock has.

Do you take it I would astonish?
Does the daylight astonish? does the early redstart twittering
    through the woods?
Do I astonish more than they?
This hour I tell things in confidence,
I might not tell everybody, but I will tell you.


### 20

Who goes there? hankering, gross, mystical, nude;
How is it I extract strength from the beef I eat?

What is a man anyhow? what am I? what are you?

All I mark as my own you shall offset it with your own,
Else it were time lost listening to me.

I do not snivel that snivel the world over,
That months are vacuums and the ground but wallow and
    filth.

Whimpering and truckling fold with powders for invalids,
    conformity goes to the fourth-remov'd,
I wear my hat as I please indoors or out.

Why should I pray? why should I venerate and be ceremo-
    nious?

Having pried through the strata, analyzed to a hair, counsel'd
    with doctors and calculated close,
I find no sweeter fat than sticks to my own bones.

In all people I see myself, none more and not one a barley-
    corn less,
And the good or bad I say of myself I say of them,
I know I am solid and sound,
To me the converging objects of the universe perpetually flow,
All are written to me, and I must get what the writing means.

I know I am deathless,
I know this orbit of mine cannot be swept by a carpenter's
    compass,
I know I shall not pass like a child's carlacue cut with a burnt
    stick at night.

I know I am august,
I do not trouble my spirit to vindicate itself or be understood,
I see that the elementary laws never apologize,
(I reckon I behave no prouder than the level I plant my house
    by, after all.)

I exist as I am, that is enough,
If no other in the world be aware I sit content,
And if each and all be aware I sit content.

One world is aware and by far the largest to me, and that is
    myself,

And whether I come to my own today or in ten thousand or
    ten million years,
I can cheerfully take it now, or with equal cheerfulness I can
    wait.

My foothold is tenon'd and mortis'd in granite,
I laugh at what you call dissolution,
And I know the amplitude of time.

21

I am the poet of the Body and I am the poet of the Soul,
The pleasures of heaven are with me and the pains of hell are
    with me,
The first I graft and increase upon myself, the latter I trans-
    late into a new tongue.
I am the poet of the woman the same as the man,
And I say it is as great to be a woman as to be a man,
And I say there is nothing greater than the mother of men.

I chant the chant of dilation or pride,
We have had ducking and deprecating about enough,
I show that size is only development.

Have you outstript the rest? are you the President?
It is a trifle, they will more than arrive there every one, and
    still pass on.

I am he that walks with the tender and growing night,
I call to the earth and sea half-held by the night.

Press close bare-bosom'd night—press close magnetic nourish-
    ing night!
Night of south winds—night of the large few stars!
Still nodding night—mad naked summer night.

Smile O voluptuous cool-breath'd earth!
Earth of the slumbering and liquid trees!
Earth of departed sunset—earth of the mountains misty-topt!
Earth of the vitreous pour of the full moon just tinged with
    blue!
Earth of shine and dark mottling the tide of the river!
Earth of the limpid gray of clouds brighter and clearer for my
    sake!
Far-swooping elbow'd earth—rich apple-blossom'd earth!
Smile, for your lover comes.

Prodigal, you have given me love—therefore I to you give
    love!
O unspeakable passionate love.

22

You sea! I resign myself to you also—I guess what you mean,
I behold from the beach your crooked inviting fingers,
I believe you refuse to go back without feeling of me,
We must have a turn together, I undress, hurry me out of
    sight of the land,
Cushion me soft, rock me in billowy drowse,
Dash me with amorous wet, I can repay you.

Sea of stretch'd ground-swells,
Sea breathing broad and convulsive breaths,
Sea of the brine of life and of unshovel'd yet always-ready
    graves,
Howler and scooper of storms, capricious and dainty sea,
I am integral with you, I too am of one phase and of all
    phases.

Partaker of influx and efflux I, extoller of hate and concilia-
    tion,
Extoller of amies[1] and those that sleep in each other's arms.

[1] Friends, as distinguished from lovers.

I am he attesting sympathy,
(Shall I make my list of things in the house and skip the house
    that supports them?)

I am not the poet of goodness only, I do not decline to be the
    poet of wickedness also.

What blurt is this about virtue and about vice?
Evil propels me and reform of evil propels me, I stand indif-
    ferent,
My gait is no fault-finder's or rejecter's gait,
I moisten the roots of all that has grown.

Did you fear some scrofula out of the unflagging pregnancy?
Did you guess the celestial laws are yet to be work'd over and
    rectified?

I find one side a balance and the antipodal side a balance,
Soft doctrine as steady help as stable doctrine,
Thoughts and deeds of the present our rouse and early start.

This minute that comes to me over the past decillions,
There is no better than it and now.

What behaved well in the past or behaves well today is not
    such a wonder,
The wonder is always and always how there can be a mean
    man or an infidel.

25

Dazzling and tremendous how quick the sun-rise would kill
    me,
If I could not now and always send sun-rise out of me.

We also ascend dazzling and tremendous as the sun,
We found our own O my soul in the calm and cool of the day-
    break.

My voice goes after what my eyes cannot reach,
With the twirl of my tongue I encompass worlds and volumes
    of worlds.

Speech is the twin of my vision, it is unequal to measure it-
    self,
It provokes me forever, it says sarcastically,
*Walt you contain enough, why don't you let it out then?*

Come now I will not be tantalized, you conceive too much of
    articulation,
Do you not know O speech how the buds beneath you are
    folded?
Waiting in gloom, protected by frost,
The dirt receding before my prophetical screams,
I underlying causes to balance them at last,
My knowledge my live parts, it keeping tally with the mean-
    ing of all things,
Happiness, (which whoever hears me let him or her set out
    in search of this day.)

My final merit I refuse you, I refuse putting from me what I
    really am,
Encompass worlds, but never try to encompass me,
I crowd your sleekest and best by simply looking toward you.

Writing and talking do not prove me,
I carry the plenum of proof and every thing else in my face,
With the hush of my lips I wholly confound the skeptic.

30

All truths wait in all things,
They neither hasten their own delivery nor resist it,
They do not need the obstetric forceps of the surgeon,
The insignificant is as big to me as any,
(What is less or more than a touch?)

Logic and sermons never convince,
The damp of the night drives deeper into my soul.


(Only what proves itself to every man and woman is so,
Only what nobody denies is so.)


A minute and a drop of me settle my brain,
I believe the soggy clods shall become lovers and lamps,
And a compend of compends is the meat of a man or woman,
And a summit and flower there is the feeling they have for
    each other,
And they are to branch boundlessly out of that lesson until it
    becomes omnific,
And until one and all shall delight us, and we them.


31

I believe a leaf of grass is no less than the journeywork of the
    stars,
And the pismire is equally perfect, and a grain of sand, and
    the egg of the wren,
And the tree-toad is a chef-d'œuvre for the highest,
And the running blackberry would adorn the parlors of
    heaven,
And the narrowest hinge in my hand puts to scorn all ma-
    chinery,
And the cow crunching with depress'd head surpasses any
    statue,
And a mouse is miracle enough to stagger sextillions of in-
    fidels.


I find I incorporate gneiss, coal, long-threaded moss, fruits,
    grains, esculent roots,
And am stucco'd with quadrupeds and birds all over,
And have distanced what is behind me for good reasons,
But call any thing back again when I desire it.

In vain the speeding or shyness,
In vain the plutonic rocks send their old heat against my ap-
     proach,
In vain the mastodon retreats beneath its own powder'd
     bones,
In vain objects stand leagues off and assume manifold shapes,
In vain the ocean settling in hollows and the great monsters
     lying low,
In vain the buzzard houses herself with the sky,
In vain the snake slides through the creepers and logs,
In vain the elk takes to the inner passes of the woods,
In vain the razor-bill'd auk sails far north to Labrador,
I follow quickly, I ascend to the nest in the fissure of the cliff.

32

I think I could turn and live with animals, they're so placid
     and self-contain'd,
I stand and look at them long and long.

They do not sweat and whine about their condition,
They do not lie awake in the dark and weep for their sins,
They do not make me sick discussing their duty to God,
Not one is dissatisfied, not one is demented with the mania of
     owning things,
Not one kneels to another, nor to his kind that lived thou-
     sands of years ago,
Not one is respectable or unhappy over the whole earth.

So they show their relations to me and I accept them,
They bring me tokens of myself, they evince them plainly in
     their possession.

I wonder where they get those tokens,
Did I pass that way huge times ago and negligently drop
     them?

Myself moving forward then and now and forever,
Gathering and showing more always and with velocity,
Infinite and omnigenous, and the like of these among them,
Not too exclusive toward the reachers of my remembrancers,
Picking out here one that I love, and now go with him on
     brotherly terms.

A gigantic beauty of a stallion, fresh and responsive to my
     caresses,
Head high in the forehead, wide between the ears,
Limbs glossy and supple, tail dusting the ground,
Eyes full of sparkling wickedness, ears finely cut, flexibly
     moving.
His nostrils dilate as my heels embrace him,
His well-built limbs tremble with pleasure as we race around
     and return.

I but use you a minute, then I resign you, stallion,
Why do I need your paces when I myself out-gallop them?
Even as I stand or sit passing faster than you.

### 35

Would you hear of an old-time sea-fight?
Would you learn who won by the light of the moon and stars?
List to the yarn, as my grandmother's father the sailor told it
     to me.

Our foe was no skulk in his ship I tell you, (said he,)
His was the surly English pluck, and there is no tougher or
     truer, and never was, and never will be;
Along the lower'd eve he came horribly raking us.

We closed with him, the yards entangled, the cannon touch'd.
My captain lash'd fast with his own hands.

We had receiv'd some eighteen pound shots under the water,
On our lower-gun-deck two large pieces had burst at the first
    fire, killing all around and blowing up overhead.


Fighting at sun-down, fighting at dark,
Ten o'clock at night, the full moon well up, our leaks on the
    gain, and five feet of water reported,
The master-at-arms loosing the prisoners confined in the after-
    hold to give them a chance for themselves.
The transit to and from the magazine is now stopt by the
    sentinels,
They see so many strange faces they do not know whom to
    trust.
Our frigate takes fire,
The other asks if we demand quarter?
If our colors are struck and the fighting done?


Now I laugh content, for I hear the voice of my little captain,
*We have not struck*, he composedly cries, *we have just begun
    our part of the fighting*.


Only three guns are in use,
One is directed by the captain himself against the enemy's
    mainmast,
Two well serv'd with grape and canister silence his musketry
    and clear his decks.


The tops alone second the fire of this little battery, especially
    the main-top,
They hold out bravely during the whole of the action.


Not a moment's cease.
The leaks gain fast on the pumps, the fire eats toward the
    powder-magazine.

One of the pumps has been shot away, it is generally thought
    we are sinking.

Serene stands the little captain,
He is not hurried, his voice is neither high nor low,
His eyes give more light to us than our battle-lanterns.

Toward twelve there in the beams of the moon they surrender
    to us.

36

Stretch'd and still lies the midnight,
Two great hulls motionless on the breast of the darkness,
Our vessel riddled and slowly sinking, preparations to pass to
    the one we have conquer'd,
The captain on the quarter-deck coldly giving his orders
    through a countenance white as a sheet,
Near by the corpse of the child that serv'd in the cabin,
The dead face of an old salt with long white hair and care-
    fully curl'd whiskers,
The flames spite of all that can be done flickering aloft and
    below,
The husky voices of the two or three officers yet fit for duty,
Formless stacks of bodies and bodies by themselves, dabs of
    flesh upon the masts and spars,
Cut of cordage, dangle of rigging, slight shock of the soothe
    of waves,
Black and impassive guns, litter of powder-parcels, strong
    scent,
A few large stars overhead, silent and mournful shining,
Delicate sniffs of sea-breeze, smells of sedgy grass and fields
    by the shore, death-messages given in charge to sur-
    vivors,
The hiss of the surgeon's knife, the gnawing teeth of his saw,
Wheeze, cluck, swash of falling blood, short wild scream, and
    long, dull, tapering groan,
These so, these irretrievable.

44

It is time to explain myself—let us stand up.

What is known I strip away,
I launch all men and women forward with me into the Unknown.

The clock indicates the moment—but what does eternity indicate?

We have thus far exhausted trillions of winters and summers,
There are trillions ahead, and trillions ahead of them.

Rise after rise bow the phantoms behind me,
Afar down I see the huge first Nothing, I know I was even there,
I waited unseen and always, and slept through the lethargic mist,
And took my time, and took no hurt from the fetid carbon.

Long I was hugg'd close—long and long.
Immense have been the preparations for me,
Faithful and friendly the arms that have help'd me.

Cycles ferried my cradle, rowing and rowing like cheerful boatmen,
For room to me stars kept aside in their own rings,
They sent influences to look after what was to hold me.

Before I was born out of my mother generations guided me,
My embryo has never been torpid, nothing could overlay it.

For it the nebula cohered to an orb,
The long slow strata piled to rest it on,
Vast vegetables gave it sustenance,

Monstrous sauroids transported it in their mouths and de-
    posited it with care.
All forces have been steadily employ'd to complete and de-
    light me,
Now on this spot I stand with my robust soul.

### 48

I have said that the soul is not more than the body,
And I have said that the body is not more than the soul,
And nothing, not God, is greater to one than one's self is,
And whoever walks a furlong without sympathy walks to his
    own funeral drest in his shroud,
And I or you pocketless of a dime may purchase the pick of
    the earth,
And to glance with an eye or show a bean in its pod con-
    founds the learning of all times,
And there is no trade or employment but the young man fol-
    lowing it may become a hero,
And there is no object so soft but it makes a hub for the
    wheel'd universe,
And I say to any man or woman, Let your soul stand cool and
    composed before a million universes.

And I say to mankind, Be not curious about God,
For I who am curious about each am not curious about God,
(No array of terms can say how much I am at peace about
    God and about death.)

I hear and behold God in every object, yet understand God
    not in the least,
Nor do I understand who there can be more wonderful than
    myself.

Why should I wish to see God better than this day?
I see something of God each hour of the twenty-four, and
    each moment then,

In the faces of men and women I see God, and in my own
    face in the glass,
I find letters from God dropt in the street, and every one is
    sign'd by God's name,
And I leave them where they are, for I know that wheresoe'er
    I go,
Others will punctually come for ever and ever.


52

The spotted hawk swoops by and accuses me, he complains
    of my gab and my loitering.


I too am not a bit tamed, I too am untranslatable,
I sound my barbaric yawp over the roofs of the world.


The last scud of day holds back for me,
It flings my likeness after the rest and true as any on the
    shadow'd wilds,
It coaxes me to the vapor and the dusk.
I depart as air, I shake my white locks at the runaway sun,
I effuse my flesh in eddies, and drift it in lacy jags.


I bequeath myself to the dirt to grow from the grass I love,
If you want me again look for me under your boot-soles.


You will hardly know who I am or what I mean,
But I shall be good health to you nevertheless,
And filter and fiber your blood.


Failing to fetch me at first keep encouraged,
Missing me one place search another,
I stop somewhere waiting for you.

## On the Beach at Night

On the beach at night,
Stands a child with her father,
Watching the east, the autumn sky.

Up through the darkness,
While ravening clouds, the burial clouds, in black masses
    spreading,
Lower sullen and fast athwart and down the sky,
Amid a transparent clear belt of ether yet left in the east,
Ascends large and calm the lord-star Jupiter,
And nigh at hand, only a very little above,
Swim the delicate sisters the Pleiades.

From the beach the child holding the hand of her father,
Those burial clouds that lower victorious soon to devour all,
Watching, silently weeps.

Weep not, child,
Weep not, my darling,
With these kisses let me remove your tears,
The ravening clouds shall not long be victorious;
They shall not long possess the sky, they devour the stars
    only in apparition,
Jupiter shall emerge, be patient, watch again another night,
    the Pleiades shall emerge,
They are immortal, all those stars both silvery and golden
    shall shine out again,
The great stars and the little ones shall shine out again, they
    endure,
The vast immortal suns and the long-enduring pensive moons
    shall again shine.

Then dearest child mournest thou only for Jupiter?
Considerest thou alone the burial of the stars?


Something there is,
(With my lips soothing thee, adding I whisper,
I give thee the first suggestion, the problem and indirection )
Something there is more immortal even than the stars,
(Many the burials, many the days and nights, passing away,)
Something that shall endure longer even than lustrous Jupiter,
Longer than sun or any revolving satellite,
Or the radiant sisters the Pleiades.


## When Lilacs Last in the Dooryard Bloom'd [1]

### 1

When lilacs last in the dooryard bloom'd,
And the great star early droop'd in the western sky in the
        night,
I mourn'd, and yet shall mourn with ever-returning spring.


Ever-returning spring, trinity sure to me you bring,
Lilac blooming perennial and drooping star in the west,
And thought of him I love.


### 2

O powerful western fallen star!
O shades of night—O moody, tearful night!
O great star disappear'd—O the black murk that hides the
        star!
O cruel hands that hold me powerless—O helpless soul of me!
O harsh surrounding cloud that will not free my soul.

[1] This and the rhymed stanzas of "O Captain! My Captain!"
which follow are part of a group entitled "Memories of President
Lincoln."

### 3

In the dooryard fronting an old farm-house near the white-
    wash'd palings,
Stands the lilac-bush tall-growing with heart-shaped leaves of
    rich green,
With many a pointed blossom rising delicate, with the per-
    fume strong I love,
With every leaf a miracle—and from this bush in the door-
    yard,
With delicate-color'd blossoms and heart-shaped leaves of
    rich green,
A sprig with its flower I break.

### 4

In the swamp in secluded recesses,
A shy and hidden bird is warbling a song.

Solitary the thrush,
The hermit withdrawn to himself, avoiding the settlements,
Sings by himself a song.

Song of the bleeding throat,
Death's outlet song of life, (for well dear brother I know,
If thou wast not granted to sing thou would'st surely die.)

### 5

Over the breast of the spring, the land, amid cities,
Amid lanes and through old woods, where lately the violets
    peep'd from the ground, spotting the gray débris,
Amid the grass in the fields each side of the lanes, passing the
    endless grass,
Passing the yellow-spear'd wheat, every grain from its shroud
    in the dark-brown fields uprisen,
Passing the apple-tree blows of white and pink in the or-
    chards,
Carrying a corpse to where it shall rest in the grave,
Night and day journeys a coffin.

6

Coffin that passes through lanes and streets,
Through day and night with the great cloud darkening the
    land,
With the pomp of the inloop'd flags with the cities draped in
    black,
With the show of the States themselves as of crape-veil'd
    women standing,
With processions long and winding and the flambeaus of the
    night,
With the countless torches lit, with the silent sea of faces and
    the unbared heads,
With the waiting depot, the arriving coffin, and the somber
    faces,
With dirges through the night, with the thousand voices ris-
    ing strong and solemn,
With all the mournful voices of the dirges pour'd around the
    coffin,
The dim-lit churches and the shuddering organs—where amid
    these you journey,
With the tolling tolling bells' perpetual clang,
Here, coffin that slowly passes,
I give you my sprig of lilac.

7

(Nor for you, for one alone,
Blossoms and branches green to coffins all I bring,
For fresh as the morning, thus would I chant a song for you
    O sane and sacred death.

All over bouquets of roses,
O death, I cover you over with roses and early lilies,
But mostly and now the lilac that blooms the first,
Copious I break, I break the sprigs from the bushes,
With loaded arms I come, pouring for you,
For you and the coffins all of you O death.)

8

O western orb sailing the heaven,
Now I know what you must have meant as a month since I
    walk'd,
As I walk'd in silence the transparent shadowy night,
As I saw you had something to tell as you bent to me night
    after night,
As you droop'd from the sky low down as if to my side, (while
    the other stars all look'd on,)
As we wander'd together the solemn night, (for something I
    know not what kept me from sleep,)
As the night advanced, and I saw on the rim of the west how
    full you were of woe,
As I stood on the rising ground in the breeze in the cool
    transparent night,
As I watch'd where you pass'd and was lost in the netherward
    black of the night,
As my soul in its trouble dissatisfied sank, as where you sad
    orb,
Concluded, dropt in the night, and was gone.

9

Sing on there in the swamp,
O singer bashful and tender, I hear your notes, I hear your
    call,
I hear, I come presently, I understand you,
But a moment I linger, for the lustrous star has detain'd me,
The star my departing comrade holds and detains me.

10

O how shall I warble myself for the dead one there I loved?
And how shall I deck my song for the large sweet soul that
    has gone?
And what shall my perfume be for the grave of him I love?

Sea-winds blown from east and west,
Blown from the Eastern sea and blown from the Western sea,
    till there on the prairies meeting,
These and with these and the breath of my chant,
I'll perfume the grave of him I love.


11

O what shall I hang on the chamber walls?
And what shall the pictures be that I hang on the walls,
To adorn the burial-house of him I love?
Pictures of growing spring and farms and homes,
With the Fourth-month eve at sundown, and the gray smoke
    lucid and bright,
With floods of the yellow gold of the gorgeous, indolent, sink-
    ing sun, burning, expanding the air,
With the fresh sweet herbage under foot, and the pale green
    leaves of the trees prolific,
In the distance the flowing glaze, the breast of the river, with
    a wind-dapple here and there,
With ranging hills on the banks, with many a line against the
    sky, and shadows,
And the city at hand, with dwellings so dense, and stacks of
    chimneys,
And all the scenes of life and the workshops, and the work-
    men homeward returning.


12

Lo, body and soul—this land,
My own Manhattan with spires, and the sparkling and hurry-
    ing tides, and the ships,
The varied and ample land, the South and the North in the
    light, Ohio's shores and flashing Missouri,
And ever the far-spreading prairies cover'd with grass and
    corn.

Lo, the most excellent sun so calm and haughty,
The violet and purple morn with just-felt breezes,
The gentle soft-born measureless light,
The miracle spreading bathing all, the fulfill'd noon,
The coming eve delicious, the welcome night and the stars,
Over my cities shining all, enveloping man and land.

13

Sing on, sing on you gray-brown bird,
Sing from the swamps, the recesses, pour your chant from
    the bushes,
Limitless out of the dusk, out of the cedars and pines.
Sing on dearest brother, warble your reedy song,
Loud human song, with voice of uttermost woe.
O liquid and free and tender!
O wild and loose to my soul—O wondrous singer!
You only I hear—yet the star holds me, (but will soon de-
    part,)
Yet the lilac with mastering odor holds me.

14

Now while I sat in the day and look'd forth,
In the close of the day with its light and the fields of spring,
    and the farmers preparing their crops,
In the large unconscious scenery of my land with its lakes
    and forests,
In the heavenly aerial beauty, (after the perturb'd winds and
    the storms,)
Under the arching heavens of the afternoon swift passing, and
    the voices of children and women,
The many-moving sea-tides, and I saw the ships how they
    sail'd,
And the summer approaching with richness, and the fields all
    busy with labor,

And the infinite separate houses, how they all went on, each
     with its meals and minutia of daily usages,
And the streets how their throbbings throbb'd, and the cities
     pent—lo, then and there,
Falling upon them all and among them all, enveloping me
     with the rest,
Appear'd the cloud, appear'd the long black trail,
And I knew death, its thought, and the sacred knowledge of
     death.

Then with the knowledge of death as walking one side of me,
And the thought of death close-walking the other side of me,
And I in the middle as with companions, and as holding the
     hands of companions,
I fled forth to the hiding receiving night that talks not,
Down to the shores of the water, the path by the swamp in
     the dimness,
To the solemn shadowy cedars and ghostly pines so still.

And the singer so shy to the rest receiv'd me,
The gray-brown bird I know receiv'd us comrades three,
And he sang the carol of death, and a verse for him I love.

From deep secluded recesses,
From the fragrant cedars and the ghostly pines so still,
Came the carol of the bird.

And the charm of the carol rapt me
As I held as if by their hands my comrades in the night,
And the voice of my spirit tallied the song of the bird.

*Come lovely and soothing death,*
*Undulate round the world, serenely arriving, arriving,*
*In the day, in the night, to all, to each,*
*Sooner or later delicate death.*

*Prais'd be the fathomless universe,*
*For life and joy, and for objects and knowledge curious,*
*And for love, sweet love—but praise! praise! praise!*
*For the sure-enwinding arms of cool-enfolding· death.*

*Dark mother always gliding near with soft feet,*
*Have none chanted for thee a chant of fullest welcome?*
*Then I chant it for thee, I glorify thee above all,*
*I bring thee a song that when thou must indeed come, come*
*    unfalteringly.*

*Approach strong deliveress,*
*When it is so, when thou hast taken them I joyously sing the*
*    dead,*
*Lost in the loving floating ocean of thee,*
*Laved in the flood of thy bliss O death.*

*From me to thee glad serenades,*
*Dances for thee I propose saluting thee, adornments and*
*    feastings for thee,*
*And the sights of the open landscape and the high-spread sky*
*    are fitting,*
*And life and the fields, and the huge and thoughtful night.*

*The night in silence under many a star,*
*The ocean shore and the husky whispering wave whose voice*
*    I know,*
*And the soul turning to thee O vast and well-veil'd death,*
*And the body gratefully nestling close to thee.*

*Over the tree-tops I float thee a song,*
*Over the rising and sinking waves, over the myriad fields and*
*    the prairies wide,*
*Over the dense-pack'd cities all and the teeming wharves and*
*    ways,*
*I float this carol with joy, with joy to thee O death.*

15

To the tally of my soul,
Loud and strong kept up the gray-brown bird,
With pure deliberate notes spreading filling the night.

Loud in the pines and cedars dim,
Clear in the freshness moist and the swamp-perfume,
And I with my comrades there in the night.

While my sight that was bound in my eyes unclosed,
As to long panoramas of visions.

And I saw askant the armies,
I saw as in noiseless dreams hundreds of battle-flags,
Borne through the smoke of the battles and pierc'd with mis-
    siles I saw them,
And carried hither and yon through the smoke, and torn and
    bloody,
And at last but a few shreds left on the staffs, (and all in si-
    lence,)
And the staffs all splinter'd and broken.

I saw battle-corpses, myriads of them,
And the white skeletons of young men, I saw them,
I saw the débris and débris of all the slain soldiers of the war,
But I saw they were not as was thought,
They themselves were fully at rest, they suffer'd not,
The living remain'd and suffer'd, the mother suffer'd,
And the wife and the child and the musing comrade suffer'd,
And the armies that remain'd suffer'd.

16

Passing the visions, passing the night,
Passing, unloosing the hold of my comrades' hands,
Passing the song of the hermit bird and the tallying song of
    my soul,
Victorious song, death's outlet song, yet varying ever-altering
    song,
As low and wailing, yet clear the notes, rising and falling,
    flooding the night,
Sadly sinking and fainting, as warning and warning, and yet
    again bursting with joy,
Covering the earth and filling the spread of the heaven,
As that powerful psalm in the night I heard from recesses,
Passing, I leave thee lilac with heart-shaped leaves,
I leave thee there in the dooryard, blooming, returning with
    spring.

I cease from my song for thee,
From my gaze on thee in the west, fronting the west, com-
    muning with thee,
O comrade lustrous with silver face in the night.

Yet each to keep and all, retrievements out of the night,
The song, the wondrous chant of the gray-brown bird,
And the tallying chant, the echo arous'd in my soul,
With the lustrous and drooping star with the countenance full
    of woe,
With the holders holding my hand nearing the call of the
    bird,
Comrades mine and I in the midst, and their memory ever to
    keep, for the dead I loved so well,
For the sweetest, wisest soul of all my days and lands—and
    this for his dear sake,
Lilac and star and bird twined with the chant of my soul,
There in the fragrant pines and the cedars dusk and dim.

## O Captain! My Captain!

O Captain! my Captain! our fearful trip is done,
The ship has weather'd every rack, the prize we sought is
 won,
The port is near, the bells I hear, the people all exulting,
While follow eyes the steady keel, the vessel grim and daring;
  But O heart! heart! heart!
   O the bleeding drops of red,
    Where on the deck my Captain lies,
    Fallen cold and dead.

O Captain! my Captain! rise up and hear the bells;
Rise up—for you the flag is flung—for you the bugle trills,
For you bouquets and ribbon'd wreaths—for you the shores
 a-crowding,
For you they call, the swaying mass, their eager faces turning;
  Here Captain! dear father!
   The arm beneath your head!
    It is some dream that on the deck,
    You've fallen cold and dead.

My Captain does not answer, his lips are pale and still,
My father does not feel my arm, he has no pulse nor will,
The ship is anchor'd safe and sound, its voyage closed and
 done,
From fearful trip the victor ship comes in with object won;
  Exult O shores, and ring O bells!
   But I with mournful tread,
    Walk the deck my Captain lies,
    Fallen cold and dead.

## *Dirge for Two Veterans*

The last sunbeam
Lightly falls from the finished Sabbath,
On the pavement here, and there beyond it is looking,
    Down a new-made double grave,

    Lo, the moon ascending,
Up from the east the silvery round moon,
Beautiful over the house-tops ghastly, phantom moon,
    Immense and silent moon.

    I see a sad procession,
And I hear the sound of coming full-key'd bugles,
All the channels of the city streets they're flooding,
    As with voices and with tears.

    I hear the great drums pounding,
And the small drums steady whirring,
And every blow of the great convulsive drums,
    Strikes me through and through.

    For the son is brought with the father,
(On the foremost ranks of the fierce assault they fell,
Two veterans son and father dropt together,
    And the double grave awaits them).

    Now nearer blow the bugles,
And the drums strike more convulsive,
And the daylight o'er the pavement quite has faded,
    And the strong dead-march enwraps me.

    In the eastern sky up-buoying,
The sorrowful vast phantom moves illumin'd,
('Tis some mother's large transparent face,
    In heaven brighter growing).

O strong dead-march, you please me!
O moon immense with your silvery face, you soothe me!
O my soldiers twain! O my veterans passing to burial!
What I have I also give you.

The moon gives you light,
And the bugles and the drums give you music,
And my heart, O my soldiers, my veterans,
My heart gives you love.

## The Poet

FROM "BY BLUE ONTARIO'S SHORE"

I listened to the Phantom by Ontario's shore,
I heard the voice arising demanding bards,
By them all native and grand, by them alone can these States
be fused into the compact organism of a Nation.

To hold men together by paper and seal or by compulsion is
no account,
That only holds men together which aggregates all in a living principle, as the hold of the limbs of the body or the
fibres of plants.

Of all races and eras these States with veins full of poetical
stuff most need poets, and are to have the greatest, and
use them the greatest,
Their Presidents shall not be their common referee so much
as their poets shall.

(Soul of love and tongue of fire!
Eye to pierce the deepest deeps and sweep the world!
Ah, Mother, prolific and full in all besides, yet how
long barren, barren?)

10

Of these States the poet is the equable man,

Not in him but off from him things are grotesque, eccentric,
      fail of their full returns,

Nothing out of its place is good, nothing in its place is bad,

He bestows on every object or quality its fit proportion,
      neither more nor less,

He is the arbiter of the diverse, he is the key,

He is the equaliser of his age and land,

He supplies what wants supplying, he checks what wants
      checking,

In peace out of him speaks the spirit of peace, large, rich,
      thrifty, building populous towns, encouraging agricul-
      ture, arts, commerce, lighting the study of man, the soul,
      health, immortality, government,

In war he is the best backer of the war, he fetches artillery
      as good as the engineer's, he can make every word he
      speaks draw blood,

The years straying toward infidelity he withholds by his
      steady faith,

He is no arguer, he is judgment (Nature accepts him abso-
      lutely),

He judges not as the judge judges but as the sun falling
      round a helpless thing,

As he sees the farthest he has the most faith,

His thoughts are the hymns of the praise of things,

In the dispute on God and eternity he is silent,

He sees eternity less like a play with a prologue and denoue-
      ment,

He sees eternity in men and women, he does not see men and
      women as dreams or dots.

For the great Idea, the idea of perfect and free individuals,

For that, the bard walks in advance, leader of leaders,

The attitude of him cheers up slaves and horrifies foreign
      despots.

Without extinction is Liberty, without retrograde is Equality,
They live in the feelings of young men and the best women,
(Not for nothing have the indomitable heads of the earth been
    always ready to fall for Liberty).


11

For the great Idea,
That, O my brethren, that is the mission of poets.


Songs of stern defiance ever ready,
Songs of the rapid arming and the march,
The flag of peace quick-folded, and instead the flag we know,
Warlike flag of the great Idea.


(Angry cloth I saw there leaping!
I stand again in leaden rain your flapping folds saluting,
I sing you over all, flying beckoning through the fight—O
    the hard-contested fight!


The cannons ope their rosy-flashing muzzles—the hurtled
    balls scream,
The battle-front forms amid the smoke—the volleys pour in-
    cessant from the line,
Hark, the ringing word *Charge!*—now the tussle and the furi-
    ous maddening yells,
Now the corpses tumble curl'd upon the ground,
Cold, cold in death, for precious life of you,
Angry cloth I saw there leaping.)


12

Are you he who would assume a place to teach or be a poet
    here in the States?
The place is august, the terms obdurate.


Who would assume to teach here may well prepare himself
    body and mind,

He may well survey, ponder, arm, fortify, harden, make lithe
    himself,
He shall surely be question'd beforehand by me with many
    and stern questions.


Who are you indeed who would talk or sing to America?
Have you studied out the land, its idioms and men?
Have you learn'd the physiology, phrenology, politics, geog-
    raphy, pride, freedom, friendship of the land? its sub-
    stratums and objects?
Have you consider'd the organic compact of the first day of
    the first year of Independence, sign'd by the Commis-
    sioners, ratified by the States, and read by Washington
    at the head of the army?
Have you possess'd yourself of the Federal Constitution?
Do you see who have left all feudal processes and poems be-
    hind them, and assumed the poems and processes of De-
    mocracy?
Are you faithful to things? do you teach what the land and
    sea, the bodies of men, womanhood, amativeness, heroic
    angers, teach?
Have you sped through fleeting customs, popularities?
Can you hold your hand against all seductions, follies, whirls,
    fierce contentions? are you very strong? are you really of
    the whole People?
Are you not of some coterie? some school or mere religion?
Are you done with reviews and criticisms of life? animating
    now to life itself?
Have you vivified yourself from the maternity of these States?
Have you too the old ever-fresh forbearance and impartiality?
Do you hold the like love for those hardening to maturity?
    for the last-born? little and big? and for the errant?


What is this you bring my America?
Is it uniform with my country?
Is it not something that has been better told or done before?

Have you not imported this or the spirit of it in some ship?

Is it not a mere tale? a rhyme? a prettiness?—is the good old
    cause in it?

Has it not dangled long at the heels of the poets, politicians,
    literats, of enemies' lands?

Does it not assume that what is notoriously gone is still here?

Does it answer universal needs? will it improve manners?

Does it sound with trumpet-voice the proud victory of the
    Union in that secession war?

Can your performance face the open fields and the seaside?

Will it absorb into me as I absorb food, air, to appear again
    in my strength, gait, face?

Have real employments contributed to it? original makers, not
    mere amanuenses?

Does it meet modern discoveries, calibres, facts, face to face?

What does it mean to American persons, progresses, cities?
    Chicago, Kanada, Arkansas?

Does it see behind the apparent custodians the real custo-
    dians standing, menacing, silent, the mechanics, Man-
    hattanese, Western men, Southerners, significant alike in
    their apathy and in the promptness of their love?

Does it see what finally befalls, and has always finally
    befallen, each temporiser, patcher, outsider, partialist,
    alarmist, infidel, who has ever ask'd anything of America?

What mocking and scornful negligence?

The track strew'd with the dust of skeletons,

By the roadside others disdainfully toss'd.


13

Rhymes and rhymers pass away, poems distill'd from poems
    pass away,

The swarms of reflectors and the polite pass, and leave ashes,

Admirers, importers, obedient persons, make but the soil of
    literature,

America justifies itself, give it time, no disguise can deceive
    it or conceal from it, it is impassive enough,

Only toward the likes of itself will it advance to meet them,
If its poets appear it will in due time advance to meet them,
    there is no fear of mistake,
(The proof of a poet shall be sternly deferr'd till his country
    absorbs him as affectionately as he has absorb'd it).

He masters whose spirit masters, he tastes sweetest who re-
    sults sweetest in the long run,
The blood of the brawn beloved of time is unconstraint;
In the need of songs, philosophy, an appropriate native grand-
    opera, shipcraft, any craft.
He or she is greatest who contributes the greatest original
    practical example.

Already a nonchalant breed, silently emerging, appears on the
    streets,
People's lips salute only doers, lovers, satisfiers, positive
    knowers,
There will shortly be no more priests, I say their work is done,
Death is without emergencies here, but life is perpetual emer-
    gencies here,
Are your body, days, manners, superb? after death you shall
    be superb,
Justice, health, self-esteem, clear the way with irresistible
    power;
How dare you place anything before a man?

14

Fall behind me States!
A man before all—myself, typical, before all.

Give me the pay I have served for,
Give me to sing the songs of the great Idea, take all the rest,
I have loved the earth, sun, animals, I have despised riches,
I have given alms to every one that ask'd, stood up for the
    stupid and crazy, devoted my income and labour to
    others,

Hated tyrants, argued not concerning God, had patience and
    indulgence toward the people, taken off my hat to noth-
    ing known or unknown,
Gone freely with powerful uneducated persons and with the
    young, and with the mothers of families,
Read these leaves to myself in the open air, tried them by
    trees, stars, rivers,
Dismiss'd whatever insulted my own soul or defiled my body,
Claim'd nothing to myself which I have not carefully claim'd
    for others on the same terms,
Sped to the camps, and comrades found and accepted from
    every State,
(Upon this breast has many a dying soldier lean'd to breathe
    his last,
This arm, this hand, this voice, have nourish'd, rais'd, re-
    stored,
To life recalling many a prostrate form);
I am willing to wait to be understood by the growth of the
    taste of myself,
Rejecting none, permitting all.

(Say, O Mother, have I not to your thought been faithful?
Have I not through life kept you and yours before me?)

15

I swear I begin to see the meaning of these things,
It is not the earth, it is not America who is so great,
It is I who am great or to be great, it is You up there, or any
    one,
It is to walk rapidly through civilisations, governments, the-
    ories,
Through poems, pageants, shows, to form individuals.

Underneath all, individuals,
I swear nothing is good to me now that ignores individuals,
The American compact is altogether with individuals,

The only government is that which makes minute of individuals,
The whole theory of the universe is directed unerringly to one
single individual—namely to You.

(Mother! with subtle sense severe, with the naked sword in
your hand,
I saw you at last refuse to treat but directly with individuals.)

16

Underneath all, Nativity,
I swear I will stand by my own nativity, pious or impious so
be it;
I swear I am charm'd with nothing except nativity,
Men, women, cities, nations, are only beautiful from nativity.

Underneath all is the Expression of love for men and women,
(I swear I have seen enough of mean and impotent modes of
expressing love for men and women,
After this day I take my own modes of expressing love for
men and women).

I swear I will have each quality of my race in myself,
(Talk as you like, he only suits these States whose manners
favour the audacity and sublime turbulence of the
States).

Underneath the lessons of things, spirits, Nature, governments, ownerships, I swear I perceive other lessons,
Underneath all to me is myself, to you yourself (the same
monotonous old song).

17

O I see flashing that this America is only you and me,
Its power, weapons, testimony, are you and me,
Its crimes, lies, thefts, defections, are you and me,

Its Congress is you and me, the officers, capitols, armies,
    ships, are you and me,
Its endless gestations of new States are you and me,
The war (that war so bloody and grim, the war I will hence-
    forth forget), was you and me,
Natural and artificial are you and me,
Freedom, language, poems, employments, are you and me,
Past, present, future, are you and me.

I dare not shirk any part of myself,
Not any part of America good or bad,
Not to build for that which builds for mankind,
Not to balance ranks, complexions, creeds, and the sexes,
Not to justify science nor the march of equality,
Nor to feed the arrogant blood of the brawn belov'd of time.

I am for those that have never been master'd,
For men and women whose tempers have never been mas-
    ter'd,
For those whom laws, theories, conventions, can never master.

I am for those who walk abreast with the whole earth,
Who inaugurate one to inaugurate all.

I will not be outfaced by irrational things,
I will penetrate what it is in them that is sarcastic upon me,
I will make cities and civilisations defer to me,
This is what I have learnt from America—it is the amount,
    and it I teach again.

(Democracy, while weapons were everywhere aim'd at your
    breast,
I saw you serenely give birth to immortal children, saw in
    dreams your dilating form,
Saw you with spreading mantle covering the world.)

## Give Me the Splendid Silent Sun

Give me the splendid silent sun with all his beams full-
    dazzling,
Give me juicy autumnal fruit ripe and red from the orchard,
Give me a field where the unmowed grass grows,
Give me an arbor, give me the trellised grape,
Give me fresh corn and wheat, give me serene-moving animals
    teaching content,
Give me nights perfectly quiet as on high plateaus west of
    the Mississippi, and I looking up at the stars,
Give me odorous at sunrise a garden of beautiful flowers
    where I can walk undisturbed,
Give me for marriage a sweet-breathed woman of whom I
    should never tire,
Give me a perfect child, give me, away aside from the noise
    of the world, a rural domestic life,
Give me to warble spontaneous songs recluse by myself, for
    my own ears only,
Give me solitude, give me Nature, give me again O Nature
    your primal sanities!
These demanding to have them, (tired with ceaseless excite-
    ment, and racked by the war-strife)
These to procure incessantly asking, rising in cries from my
    heart,
While yet incessantly asking still I adhere to my city,
Day upon day and year upon year, O city, walking your
    streets,
Where you hold me enchained a certain time refusing to give
    me up,
Yet giving to make me glutted, enriched of soul, you give me
    forever faces;
(O I see what I sought to escape, confronting, reversing my
    cries,
I see my own soul trampling down what it asked for.)

Keep your splendid silent sun,

Keep your woods, O Nature, and the quiet places by the woods,

Keep your fields of clover and timothy, and your cornfields and orchards,

Keep the blossoming buckwheat fields where the Ninth-month bees hum;

Give me faces and streets—give me these phantoms incessant and endless along the trottoirs!

Give me interminable eyes—give me women—give me comrades and lovers by the thousand!

Let me see new ones every day—let me hold new ones by the hand every day!

Give me such shows—give me the streets of Manhattan!

Give me Broadway, with the soldiers marching—give me the sound of the trumpets and drums!

(The soldiers in companies or regiments—some starting away flushed and reckless,

Some, their time up, returning with thinned ranks, young, yet very old, worn, marching, noticing nothing;)

Give me the shores and wharves heavy-fringed with black ships!

O such for me! O an intense life, full of repletion and varied!

The life of the theatre, bar-room, huge hotel, for me!

The saloon of the steamer! The crowded excursion for me! The torchlight procession!

The dense brigade bound for the war, with high-piled military wagons following;

People, endless, streaming, with strong voices, passions, pageants,

Manhattan streets with their powerful throbs, with beating drums as now,

The endless and noisy chorus, the rustle and clank of muskets (even the sight of the wounded),

Manhattan crowds, with their turbulent musical chorus!

Manhattan faces and eyes forever for me.

## To a Locomotive in Winter

Thee for my recitative,
Thee in the driving storm even as now, the snow, the winter-
　　day declining,
Thee in thy panoply, thy measur'd dual throbbing and thy
　　beat convulsive,
Thy black cylindric body, golden brass and silvery steel,
Thy ponderous side-bars, parallel and connecting rods, gyrat-
　　ing, shuttling at thy sides,
Thy metrical, now swelling pant and roar, now tapering in
　　the distance,
Thy great protruding head-light fix'd in front,
Thy long, pale, floating vapor-pennants, tinged with delicate
　　purple,
The dense and murky clouds out-belching from thy smoke-
　　stack,
Thy knitted frame, thy springs and valves, the tremulous
　　twinkle of thy wheels,
Thy train of cars behind, obedient, merrily following,
Through gale or calm, now swift, now slack, yet steadily
　　careering;
Type of the modern—emblem of motion and power—pulse
　　of the continent,
For once come serve the Muse and merge in verse, even as
　　here I see thee,
With storm and buffeting gusts of wind and falling snow,
By day thy warning ringing bell to sound its notes,
By night thy silent signal lamps to swing.

Fierce-throated beauty!
Roll through my chant with all thy lawless music, thy swing-
　　ing lamps at night,
Thy madly-whistled laughter, echoing, rumbling like an earth-
　　quake, rousing all,

Law of thyself complete, thine own track firmly holding,
(No sweetness debonair of tearful harp or glib piano thine,)
Thy trills of shrieks by rocks and hills return'd,
Launch'd o'er the prairies wide, across the lakes,
To the free skies unpent and glad and strong.


## When I Heard the Learned Astronomer

When I heard the learned astronomer,
When the proofs, the figures, were ranged in columns before
    me,
When I was shown the charts and diagrams, to add, divide,
    and measure them,
When I sitting heard the astronomer where he lectured with
    much applause in the lecture-room,
How soon unaccountable I became tired and sick,
Till rising and gliding out I wandered off by myself,
In the mystical moist night-air, and from time to time,
Looked up in perfect silence at the stars.


## The Last Invocation

At the last, tenderly,
From the walls of the powerful fortress'd house,
From the clasp of the knitted locks, from the keep of the well-
    closed doors,
Let me be wafted.

Let me glide noiselessly forth;
With the key of softness unlock the locks—with a whisper,
Set ope the doors O soul.

Tenderly—be not impatient,
(Strong is your hold O mortal flesh.
Strong is your hold O love.)

# FREDERICK GODDARD TUCKERMAN    1821–1873

## Under the Mountain

Under the mountain, as when first I knew
Its low black roof, and chimney creeper-twined,
The red house stands; and yet my footsteps find,
Vague in the walks, waste balm and feverfew.
But they are gone: no soft-eyed sisters trip
Across the porch or lintels, where, behind,
The mother sat,—sat knitting with pursed lip.
The house stands vacant in its green recess,
Absent of beauty as a broken heart;
The wild rain enters; and the sunset wind
Sighs in the chambers of their loveliness,
Or shakes the pane; and in the silent noons
The glass falls from the window, part by part,
And ringeth faintly in the grassy stones.

## And So the Day Drops By

And so the day drops by; the horizon draws
The fading sun, and we stand struck in grief,
Failing to find our haven of relief—
Wide of the way, nor sure to turn or pause,
And weep to view how fast the splendour wanes
And scarcely heed that yet some share remains
Of the red after-light, some time to mark,
Some space between the sundown and the dark.
But not for him those golden calms succeed
Who while the day is high and glory reigns
Sees it go by—as the dim pampas plain,
Hoary with salt and gray with bitter weed,
Sees the vault blacken, feels the dark wind strain,
Hears the dry thunder roll, and knows no rain.

THOMAS BUCHANAN READ                          1822–1872

### Sheridan's Ride

Up from the south, at break of day,
Bringing to Winchester fresh dismay,
The affrighted air with a shudder bore,
Like a herald in haste to the chieftain's door,
The terrible grumble, and rumble, and roar,
Telling the battle was on once more,
    And Sheridan twenty miles away.

And wider still those billows of war
Thunder'd along the horizon's bar;
And louder yet into Winchester roll'd
The roar of that red sea uncontroll'd,
Making the blood of the listener cold,
As he thought of the stake in that fiery fray,
    And Sheridan twenty miles away.

But there is a road from Winchester town,
A good broad highway leading down;
And there, through the flush of the morning light,
A steed as black as the steeds of night
Was seen to pass, as with eagle flight,
As if he knew the terrible need;
He stretch'd away with his utmost speed;
Hills rose and fell; but his heart was gay,
    With Sheridan fifteen miles away.

Still sprang from those swift hoofs, thundering south,
The dust, like smoke from the cannon's mouth,
Or the trail of a comet sweeping faster and faster,
Foreboding to traitors the doom of disaster.
The heart of the steed and the heart of the master
Were beating like prisoners assaulting their walls,
Impatient to be where the battle-field calls;

Every nerve of the charger was stain'd to full play,
  With Sheridan only ten miles away.

Under his spurning feet, the road
Like an arrowy Alpine river flow'd
And the landscape sped away behind
Like an ocean flying before the wind:
And the steed, like a bark fed with furnace ire,
Swept on, with his wild eye full of fire.
But, lo! he is nearing his heart's desire;
He is snuffing the smoke of the roaring fray,
  With Sheridan only five miles away.

The first that the general saw were the groups
Of stragglers, and then the retreating troops;
What was done? what to do? a glance told him both.
Then striking his spurs with a terrible oath,
He dash'd down the line, 'mid a storm of huzzas,
And the wave of retreat check'd its course there, because
The sight of the master compell'd it to pause.
With foam and with dust the black charger was gray;
By the flash of his eye, and the red nostril's play
He seem'd to the whole great army to say,
"I have brought you Sheridan all the way
  From Winchester down, to save the day."

Hurrah! hurrah for Sheridan!
Hurrah! hurrah for horse and man!
And when their statues are placed on high,
Under the dome of the Union sky,
The American soldier's Temple of Fame,
There with the glorious general's name
Be it said, in letters both bold and bright:
"Here is the steed that saved the day
By carrying Sheridan into the fight,
  From Winchester—twenty miles away!"

# GEORGE HENRY BOKER                    1823–1890

## *The Black Regiment*
### MAY 27TH, 1863

Dark as the clouds of even,
Ranked in the western heaven,
Waiting the breath that lifts
All the dead mass, and drifts
Tempest and falling brand
Over a ruined land;—
So still and orderly,
Arm to arm, knee to knee,
Waiting the great event,
Stands the black regiment.

Down the long dusky line
Teeth gleam and eyeballs shine;
And the bright bayonet,
Bristling and firmly set,
Flashed with a purpose grand,
Long ere the sharp command
Of the fierce rolling drum
Told them their time had come,
Told them what work was sent
For the black regiment.

"Now," the flag-sergeant cried,
"Though death and hell betide,
Let the whole nation see
If we are fit to be
Free in this land; or bound
Down, like the whining hound—
Bound with red stripes of pain
In our cold chains again!"

Oh! what a shout there went
From the black regiment!

"Charge!" Trump and drum awoke;
Onward the bondmen broke;
Bayonet and sabre-stroke
Vainly opposed their rush.
Through the wild battle's crush,
With but one thought aflush,
Driving their lords like chaff,
In the guns' mouths they laugh;
Or at the slippery brands
Leaping with open hands,
Down they tear man and horse,
Down in their awful course;
Trampling with bloody heel
Over the crashing steel;—
All their eyes forward bent,
Rushed the black regiment.

"Freedom!" their battle-cry—
"Freedom! or leave to die!"
Ah! and they meant the word,
Not as with us 'tis heard,
Not a mere party shout;
They gave their spirits out,
Trusted the end to God,
And on the gory sod
Rolled in triumphant blood.
Glad to strike one free blow,
Whether for weal or woe;
Glad to breathe one free breath,
Though on the lips of death;
Praying—alas! in vain!—
That they might fall again,

So they could once more see
That burst to liberty!
This was what "freedom" lent
To the black regiment.

Hundreds on hundreds fell;
But they are resting well;
Scourges and shackles strong
Never shall do them wrong.
Oh, to the living few,
Soldiers, be just and true!
Hail them as comrades tried;
Fight with them side by side;
Never, in field or tent,
Scorn the black regiment!

## Dirge for a Soldier

Close his eyes; his work is done.
  What to him is friend or foeman,
Rise of moon, or set of sun,
  Hand of man, or kiss of woman?
    Lay him low, lay him low,
    In the clover or the snow.
    What cares he? he cannot know:
      Lay him low!

As man may, he fought his fight,
  Proved his truth by his endeavor;
Let him sleep in solemn night,
  Sleep forever and forever.
    Lay him low, lay him low,
    In the clover or the snow!
    What cares he? he cannot know:
      Lay him low!

Fold him in his country's stars,
    Roll the drum and fire the volley!
What to him are all our wars,
    What but death bemocking folly?
        Lay him low, lay him low,
        In the clover or the snow!
        What cares he? he cannot know:
            Lay him low!

Leave him to God's watching eye,
    Trust him to the hand that made him;
Mortal love weeps idly by:
    God alone has power to aid him.
        Lay him low, lay him low,
        In the clover or the snow!
        What cares he? he cannot know:
            Lay him low!

# HENRY TIMROD                                    1829–1867

## Ode

SUNG ON THE OCCASION OF DECORATING THE GRAVES OF THE CON-
FEDERATE DEAD, AT MAGNOLIA CEMETERY, CHARLESTON, S.C., 1867

Sleep sweetly in your humble graves,
   Sleep, martyrs of a fallen cause;
Though yet no marble column craves
   The pilgrim here to pause.

In seeds of laurel in the earth
   The blossom of your fame is blown,
And somewhere, waiting for its birth,
   The shaft is in the stone!

Meanwhile, behalf the tardy years
   Which keep in trust your storied tombs,
Behold! your sisters bring their tears,
   And these memorial blooms.

Small tributes! But your shades will smile
   More proudly on these wreaths to-day,
Then when some cannon-moulded pile
   Shall overlook this bay.

Stoop, angels, hither from the skies!
   There is no holier spot of ground
Than where defeated valor lies,
   By mourning beauty crowned!

PAUL HAMILTON HAYNE                     1830–1886

## The Mocking Bird

A golden pallor of voluptuous light
Filled the warm southern night:
The moon, clear orbed, above the sylvan scene
Moved like a stately queen.
So rife with conscious beauty all the while,
What could she do but smile
At her own perfect loveliness below,
Glassed in the tranquil flow
Of crystal fountains and unruffled streams?
Half lost in waking dreams,
As down the loneliest forest dell I strayed,
Lo! from a neighboring glade,
Flashed through the drifts of moonshine, swiftly came
A fairy shape of flame.
It rose in dazzling spirals overhead,
Whence to wild sweetness wed,
Poured marvellous melodies, silvery trill on trill;
The very leaves grew still
On the charmed trees to hearken; while for me,
Heart-trilled to ecstasy,
I followed—followed the bright shape that flew,
Still circling up the blue,
Till, as a fountain that has reached its height
Falls back in sprays of light
Slowly dissolved, so that enrapturing lay
Divinely melts away
Through tremulous spaces to a music-mist,
Soon by the fitful breeze
How gently kissed
Into remote and tender silences.

EMILY DICKINSON                          1830–1886

### I'm Nobody! Who Are You?

I'm nobody! Who are you?
Are you nobody, too?
Then there's a pair of us—don't tell!
They'd banish us, you know.

How dreary to be somebody!
How public, like a frog
To tell your name the livelong day
To an admiring bog!

### I Taste a Liquor Never Brewed

I taste a liquor never brewed,
From tankards scooped in pearl;
Not all the vats upon the Rhine
Yield such an alcohol!

Inebriate of air am I,
And debauchee of dew,
Reeling, through endless summer days,
From inns of molten blue.

When landlords turn the drunken bee
Out of the foxglove's door,
When butterflies renounce their drams,
I shall but drink the more!

Till seraphs swing their snowy hats,
And saints to windows run,
To see the little tippler
Leaning against the sun!

### Of All the Souls that Stand Create

Of all the souls that stand create
I have elected one.
When sense from spirit files away,
And subterfuge is done;

When that which is and that which was
Apart, intrinsic, stand,
And this brief tragedy of flesh
Is shifted like a sand;

When figures show their royal front
And mists are carved away,—
Behold the atom I preferred
To all the lists of clay!

### Hope Is the Thing with Feathers

Hope is the thing with feathers
That perches in the soul,
And sings the tune without the words,
And never stops at all,

And sweetest in the gale is heard;
And sore must be the storm
That could abash the little bird
That kept so many warm.

I've heard it in the chillest land,
And on the strangest sea;
Yet, never, in extremity,
It asked a crumb of me.

## I Never Saw a Moor

I never saw a moor,
I never saw the sea;
Yet know I how the heather looks,
And what a wave must be.

I never spoke with God,
Nor visited in Heaven;
Yet certain am I of the spot
As if the chart were given.

## The Wind Took up the Northern Things

The wind took up the northern things
And piled them in the south,
Then bent the east unto the west
And, opening his mouth,

The four divisions of the earth
Did make as to devour,
While everything to corners slunk
Behind the awful power.

The wind unto his chambers went,
And nature ventured out,
Her subjects scattered into place,
Her systems ranged about;

Again the smoke from dwellings rose
The day abroad was heard.
How intimate, a tempest past,
The transport of the bird!

### Elysium Is as Far

Elysium is as far as to
The very nearest room,
If in that room a friend await
Felicity or doom.

What fortitude the soul contains,
That it can so endure
The accent of a coming foot,
The opening of a door.

### The Mountains Stood in Haze

The mountains stood in haze,
The valleys stopped below,
And went or waited as they liked
The river and the sky.

At leisure was the sun,
His interests of fire
A little from remark withdrawn.
The twilight spoke the spire.

So soft upon the scene
The act of evening fell
We felt how neighborly a thing
Was the invisible.

## I Dreaded that First Robin So

I dreaded that first robin so,
But he is mastered now,
And I'm accustomed to him grown—
He hurts a little, though.

I thought if I could only live
Till that first shout got by,
Not all pianos in the woods
Had power to mangle me.

I dared not meet the daffodils,
For fear their yellow gown
Would pierce me with a fashion
So foreign to my own.

I wished the grass would hurry,
So when 'twas time to see,
He'd be too tall, the tallest one
Could stretch to look at me.

I could not bear the bees should come,
I wished they'd stay away
In those dim countries where they go:
What word had they for me?

They're here, though; not a creature failed,
No blossom stayed away
In gentle deference to me,
The Queen of Calvary.

Each one salutes me as he goes,
And I my childish plumes
Lift, in bereaved acknowledgment
Of their unthinking drums.

## There Came a Day at Summer's Full

There came a day at summer's full
Entirely for me;
I thought that such were for the saints,
Where revelations be.

The sun, as common, went abroad,
The flowers, accustomed, blew,
As if no soul the solstice passed
That maketh all things new.

The time was scarce profaned by speech;
The symbol of a word
Was needless, as at sacrament
The wardrobe of our Lord.

Each was to each the sealed church,
Permitted to commune this time,
Lest we too awkward show
At supper of the Lamb.

The hours slid fast, as hours will,
Clutched tight by greedy hands;
So faces on two decks look back,
Bound to opposing lands.

And so, when all the time had failed,
Without external sound,
Each bound the other's crucifix,
We gave no other bond.

Sufficient troth that we shall rise—
Depoed, at length, the grave—
To that new marriage, justified
Through Calvaries of Love!

## I Thought the Train Would Never Come

I thought the train would never come.
How slow the whistle sang!
I don't believe a peevish bird
So whimpered for the spring.

I taught my heart a hundred times
Precisely what to say—
Provoking lover, when you came
Its treatise flew away!

To hide my strategy, too late,
To wiser grow, too soon,
For miseries so halcyon
The happiness atone.

## Success Is Counted Sweetest

Success is counted sweetest
By those who ne'er succeed.
To comprehend a nectar
Requires sorest need.

Not one of all the purple host
Who took the flag today
Can tell the definition
So clear, of victory,

As he, defeated, dying,
On whose forbidden ear
The distant strains of triumph
Break, agonized and clear.

## I Had Been Hungry All the Years

I had been hungry all the years;
My noon had come, to dine;
I, trembling, drew the table near,
And touched the curious wine.

'Twas this on tables I had seen,
When turning, hungry, lone,
I looked in windows, for the wealth
I could not hope to own.

I did not know the ample bread,
'Twas so unlike the crumb
The birds and I had often shared
In nature's dining-room.

The plenty hurt me, 'twas so new—
Myself felt ill and odd,
As berry of a mountain bush
Transplanted to the road.

Now was I hungry; so I found
That hunger was a way
Of persons outside windows,
The entering takes away.

## Because I Could Not Stop for Death

Because I could not stop for Death,
He kindly stopped for me;
The carriage held but just ourselves
And Immortality.

We slowly drove, he knew no haste,
And I had put away
My labour, and my leisure too,
For his civility.

We passed the school where children played
Their lessons scarcely done;
We passed the fields of gazing grain,
We passed the setting sun.

We paused before a house that seemed
A swelling on the ground;
The roof was scarcely visible,
The cornice but a mound.

Since then 'tis centuries; but each
Feels shorter than the day
I first surmised the horses' heads
Were toward eternity.

## THOMAS BAILEY ALDRICH                    1836–1907

### Memory

My mind lets go a thousand things,
Like dates of wars and deaths of kings,
And yet recalls the very hour—
'Twas noon by yonder village tower,
And on the last blue noon in May
The wind came briskly up this way,
Crisping the brook beside the road;
Then, pausing here, set down its load
Of pine-scents, and shook listlessly
Two petals from that wild-rose tree.

### Enamored Architect of Airy Rhyme

Enamored architect of airy rhyme,
Build as thou wilt; heed not what each man says:
Good souls, but innocent of dreamers' ways,
Will come, and marvel why thou wastest time;
Others, beholding how thy turrets climb
'Twixt theirs and heaven, will hate thee all thy days;
But most beware of those who come to praise.
O Wondersmith, O worker in sublime
And heaven-sent dreams, let art be all in all;
Build as thou wilt, unspoiled by praise or blame,
Build as thou wilt, and as thy light is given:
Then, if at last the airy structure fall,
Dissolve, and vanish—take thyself no shame.
They fail, and they alone, who have not striven.

# BRET HARTE                                    1839–1902

## *What the Bullet Sang*

O joy of creation
    To be!
O rapture to fly
    And be free!
Be the battle lost or won,
Though its smoke shall hide the sun,
I shall find my love—the one
    Born for me!

I shall know him where he stands,
    All alone,
With the power in his hands
    Not o'erthrown;
I shall know him by his face,
By his god-like front and grace;
I shall hold him for a space,
    All my own!

It is he—O my love!
    So bold!
It is I—All thy love
    Foretold!
It is I, O love! what bliss!
Dost thou answer to my kiss?
O sweetheart! what is this
    Lieth there so cold?

## *The Aged Stranger*

### AN INCIDENT OF THE WAR

"I was with Grant—" the stranger said;
    Said the farmer, "Say no more,
But rest thee here at my cottage porch,
    For thy feet are weary and sore."

"I was with Grant—" the stranger said;
    Said the farmer, "Nay, no more,—
I prithee sit at my frugal board,
    And eat of my humble store.

"How fares my boy,—my soldier boy,
    Of the old Ninth Army Corps?
I warrant he bore him gallantly
    In the smoke and the battle's roar!"

"I know him not," said the aged man,
    "And, as I remarked before,
I was with Grant—" "Nay, nay, I know,"
    Said the farmer, "say no more:

"He fell in battle,—I see, alas!
    Thou'dst smooth these tidings o'er,—
Nay, speak the truth, whatever it be,
    Though it rend my bosom's core.

"How fell he?—with his face to the foe,
    Upholding the flag he bore?
Oh, say not that my boy disgraced
    The uniform that he wore!"

"I cannot tell," said the aged man,
    "And should have remarked before,
That I was with Grant,—in Illinois,—
    Some three years before the war."

Then the farmer spake him never a word,
    But beat with his fist full sore
That aged man, who had worked for Grant
    Some three years before the war.

EDWARD ROWLAND SILL 1841–1887

## The Fool's Prayer

The royal feast was done; the King
 Sought some new sport to banish care,
And to his jester cried: "Sir Fool,
 Kneel now, and make for us a prayer!"

The jester doffed his cap and bells,
 And stood the mocking court before;
They could not see the bitter smile
 Behind the painted grin he wore.

He bowed his head, and bent his knee
 Upon the monarch's silken stool;
His pleading voice arose: "O Lord,
 Be merciful to me, a fool!

"No pity, Lord, could change the heart
 From red with wrong to white as wool;
The rod must heal the sin: but, Lord,
 Be merciful to me, a fool!

" 'Tis not by guilt the onward sweep
 Of truth and right, O Lord, we stay;
'Tis by our follies that so long
 We hold the earth from heaven away.

"These clumsy feet, still in the mire,
 Go crushing blossoms without end;
These hard, well-meaning hands we thrust
 Among the heart-strings of a friend.

"The ill-timed truth we might have kept—
 Who knows how sharp it pierced and stung?
The word we had not sense to say—
 Who knows how grandly it had rung?

"Our faults no tenderness should ask,
   The chastening stripes must cleanse them all;
But for our blunders—oh, in shame
   Before the eyes of heaven we fall.

"Earth bears no balsam for mistakes;
   Men crown the knave, and scourge the tool
That did his will; but Thou, O Lord,
   Be merciful to me, a fool!"

The room was hushed; in silence rose
   The King, and sought his gardens cool,
And walked apart, and murmured low,
   "Be merciful to me, a fool!"

## Opportunity

This I beheld, or dreamed it in a dream:
There spread a cloud of dust along a plain;
And underneath the cloud, or in it, raged
A furious battle, and men yelled, and swords
Shocked upon swords and shields. A prince's banner
Wavered, then staggered backward, hemmed by foes.
A craven hung along the battle's edge,
And thought, "Had I a sword of keener steel—
That blue blade that the king's son bears—but this
Blunt thing—!" he snapt and flung it from his hand,
And cowering crept away and left the field.

Then came the king's son, wounded, sore bestead,
And weaponless, and saw the broken sword,
Hilt-buried in the dry and trodden sand,
And ran and snatched it, and with battle shout
Lifted afresh he hewed his enemy down,
And saved a great cause that heroic day.

SIDNEY LANIER                                                    1842–1881

## The Marshes of Glynn

Glooms of the live-oaks, beautiful-braided and woven
With intricate shades of the vines that myriad-cloven
  Clamber the forks of the multiform boughs,—
      Emerald twilights,—
      Virginal shy lights,
Wrought of the leaves to allure to the whisper of vows,
When lovers pace timidly down through the green colonnades
Of the dim sweet woods, of the dear dark woods,
  Of the heavenly woods and glades,
That run to the radiant marginal sand-beach within
    The wide sea-marshes of Glynn;—

Beautiful glooms, soft dusks in the noon-day fire,—
Wildwood privacies, closets of lone desire,
Chamber from chamber parted with wavering arras of
      leaves,—
Cells for the passionate pleasure of prayer to the soul that
      grieves,
Pure with a sense of the passing of saints through the wood,
Cool for the dutiful weighing of ill with good;—
O braided dusks of the oak and woven shades of the vine,
While the riotous noon-day sun of the June-day long did shine
Ye held me fast in your heart and I held you fast in mine;
But now when the noon is no more, and riot is rest,
And the sun is a-wait at the ponderous gate of the West,
And the slant yellow beam down the wood-aisle doth seem
Like a lane into heaven that leads from a dream,—
Ay, now, when my soul all day hath drunken the soul of the
      oak,
And my heart is at ease from men, and the wearisome sound
      of the stroke

Of the scythe of time and the trowel of trade is low,
  And belief overmasters doubt, and I know that I know,
  And my spirit is grown to a lordly great compass within,
That the length and the breadth and the sweep of the marshes
    of Glynn
Will work me no fear like the fear they have wrought me of
    yore
When length was fatigue, and when breadth was but bitter-
    ness sore,
And when terror and shrinking and dreary unnamable pain
Drew over me out of the merciless miles of the plain,—


Oh, now, unafraid, I am fain to face
  The vast sweet visage of space.
To the edge of the wood I am drawn, I am drawn,
Where the gray beach glimmering runs, as a belt of the dawn,
  For a mete and a mark
    To the forest-dark:—
      So:
Affable live-oak, leaning low,—
Thus—with your favor—soft, with a reverent hand
(Not lightly touching your person, Lord of the land!),
Bending your beauty aside, with a step I stand
On the firm-packed sand,
      Free
By a world of marsh that borders a world of sea.


  Sinuous southward and sinuous northward the shimmering
    band
  Of the sand-beach fastens the fringe of the marsh to the
    folds of the land.
Inward and outward to northward and southward the beach-
    lines linger and curl
As a silver-wrought garment that clings to and follows the
    firm sweet limbs of a girl.

Vanishing, swerving, evermore curving again into sight,
Softly the sand-beach wavers away to a dim gray looping of
    light.
And what if behind me to westward the wall of the woods
    stands high?
The world lies east: how ample, the marsh and the sea and the
    sky!
A league and a league of marsh-grass, waist-high, broad in the
    blade,
Green, and all of a height, and unflecked with a light or a
    shade,
Stretch leisurely off, in a pleasant plain,
To the terminal blue of the main.

Oh, what is abroad in the marsh and the terminal sea?
  Somehow my soul seems suddenly free
From the weighing of fate and the sad discussion of sin,
By the length and the breadth and the sweep of the marshes
    of Glynn.

Ye marshes, how candid and simple and nothing-withholding
    and free
Ye publish yourselves to the sky and offer yourselves to the
    sea!
Tolerant plains, that suffer the sea and the rains and the sun,
Ye spread and span like the catholic man who hath mightily
    won
God out of knowledge and good out of infinite pain
And sight out of blindness and purity out of a stain.

As the marsh-hen secretly builds on the watery sod,
Behold I will build me a nest on the greatness of God:
I will fly in the greatness of God as the marsh-hen flies
In the freedom that fills all the space 'twixt the marsh and the
    skies:
By so many roots as the marsh-grass sends in the sod
I will heartily lay me a-hold on the greatness of God:

Oh, like to the greatness of God is the greatness within
The range of the marshes, the liberal marshes of Glynn.

And the sea lends large, as the marsh: lo, out of his plenty the
    sea
Pours fast: full soon the time of the flood-tide must be:
Look how the grace of the sea doth go
About and about through the intricate channels that flow
    Here and there,
        Everywhere,
Till his waters have flooded the uttermost creeks and the low-
    lying lanes,
And the marsh is meshed with a million veins,
That like as with rosy and silvery essences flow
In the rose-and-silver evening glow.

      Farewell, my lord Sun!
The creeks overflow: a thousand rivulets run
'Twixt the roots of the sod; the blades of the marsh-grass stir;
Passeth a hurrying sound of wings that westward whirr;
Passeth, and all is still; and the currents cease to run;
And the sea and the marsh are one.
How still the plains of the waters be!
The tide in his ecstasy.
The tide is at his highest height:
      And it is night.

And now from the Vast of the Lord will the waters of sleep
Roll in on the souls of men,
But who will reveal to our waking ken
The forms that swim and the shapes that creep
    Under the waters of sleep?
And I would I could know what swimmeth below when the
    tide comes in
On the length and breadth of the marvelous marshes of
    Glynn.

EMMA LAZARUS                                    1849–1887

## The New Colossus

INSCRIBED ON THE STATUE OF LIBERTY

Not like the brazen giant of Greek fame,
With conquering limbs astride from land to land;
Here at our sea-washed sunset gates shall stand
A mighty woman with a torch, whose flame
Is the imprisoned lightning, and her name
Mother of Exiles. From her beacon-hand
Glows world-wide welcome; her mild eyes command
The air-bridged harbor that twin cities frame.
"Keep, ancient lands, your storied pomp!" cries she
With silent lips. "Give me your tired, your poor,
Your huddled masses yearning to breathe free,
The wretched refuse of your teeming shore.
Send these, the homeless, tempest-tost to me.
I lift my lamp beside the golden door!"

EDWIN MARKHAM                                      1852–1940

### Lincoln, the Man of the People

When the Norn Mother saw the Whirlwind Hour
Greatening and darkening as it hurried on,
She left the Heaven of Heroes and came down
To make a man to meet the mortal need.
She took the tried clay of the common road—
Clay warm yet with the ancient heat of Earth,
Dashed through it all a strain of prophecy;
Tempered the heap with thrill of human tears;
Then mixed a laughter with the serious stuff.
Into the shape she breathed a flame to light
That tender, tragic, ever-changing face.
Here was a man to hold against the world,
A man to match the mountains and the sea.

The color of the ground was in him, the red earth;
The smell and smack of elemental things:
The rectitude and patience of the cliff;
The good-will of the rain that loves all leaves;
The friendly welcome of the wayside well;
The courage of the bird that dares the sea;
The gladness of the wind that shakes the corn;
The mercy of the snow that hides all scars;
The secrecy of streams that make their way
Beneath the mountain to the rifted rock;
The undelaying justice of the light
That gives as freely to the shrinking flower
As to the great oak flaring to the wind—
To the grave's low hill as to the Matterhorn
That shoulders out the sky.

Sprung from the West,
The strength of virgin forests braced his mind,
The hush of spacious prairies stilled his soul.
Up from log cabin to the Capitol,
One fire on his spirit, one resolve—
To send the keen ax to the root of wrong,
Clearing a free way for the feet of God.
And evermore he burned to do his deed
With the fine stroke and gesture of a king:
He built the rail-pile as he built the State,
Pouring his splendid strength through every blow,
The conscience of him testing every stroke,
To make his deed the measure of a man.

So came the Captain with the thinking heart;
And when the judgment thunders split the house,
Wrenching the rafters from their ancient rest,
He held the ridgepole up, and spiked again
The rafters of the Home. He held his place—
Held the long purpose like a growing tree—
Held on through blame and faltered not at praise.
And when he fell in whirlwind, he went down
As when a lordly cedar, green with boughs,
Goes down with a great shout upon the hills,
And leaves a lonesome place against the sky.

## The Man with the Hoe

WRITTEN AFTER SEEING MILLET'S WORLD-FAMOUS PAINTING

Bowed by the weight of centuries he leans
Upon his hoe and gazes on the ground,
The emptiness of ages in his face,
And on his back the burden of the world.
Who made him dead to rapture and despair,
A thing that grieves not and that never hopes,
Stolid and stunned, a brother to the ox?
Who loosened and let down this brutal jaw?
Whose was the hand that slanted back this brow?
Whose breath blew out the light within this brain?

Is this the Thing the Lord God made and gave
To have dominion over sea and land;
To trace the stars and search the heavens for power;
To feel the passion of Eternity?
Is this the dream He dreamed who shaped the suns
And marked their ways upon the ancient deep?
Down all the caverns of Hell to their last gulf
There is no shape more terrible than this—
More tongued with censure of the world's blind greed—
More filled with signs and portents for the soul—
More packed with danger to the universe.

What gulfs between him and the seraphim!
Slave of the wheel of labor, what to him
Are Plato and the swing of Pleiades?
What the long reaches of the peaks of song,
The rift of dawn, the reddening of the rose?
Through this dread shape the suffering ages look;
Time's tragedy is in that aching stoop;
Through this dread shape humanity betrayed,

Plundered, profaned, and disinherited,
Cries protest to the Judges of the World,
A protest that is also prophecy.

O masters, lords and rulers in all lands,
Is this the handiwork you give to God,
This monstrous thing distorted and soul-quenched?
How will you ever straighten up this shape;
Touch it again with immortality;
Give back the upward looking and the light;
Rebuild in it the music and the dream;
Make right the immemorial infamies,
Perfidious wrongs, immedicable woes?

O masters, lords and rulers in all lands,
How will the Future reckon with this man?
How answer his brute question in that hour
When whirlwinds of rebellion shake all shores?
How will it be with kingdoms and with kings—
With those who shaped him to the thing he is—
When this dumb terror shall rise to judge the world,
After the silence of the centuries?

## LIZETTE WOODWORTH REESE                    1856–1935

### Spicewood

The spicewood burns along the gray, spent sky,
In moist unchimneyed places, in a wind,
That whips it all before, and all behind,
Into one thick, rude flame, now low, now high.
It is the first, the homeliest thing of all—
At sight of it, that lad that by it fares,
Whistles afresh his foolish, town-caught airs—
A thing so honey-colored and so tall!

It is as though the young Year, ere he pass
To the white riot of the cherry tree,
Would fain accustom us, or here, or there,
To his new sudden ways with bough and grass,
So starts with what is humble, plain to see,
And all familiar as a cup, a chair.

# EDWIN ARLINGTON ROBINSON          1869–1935

## *Eros Turannos*

She fears him, and will always ask
    What fated her to choose him;
She meets in his engaging mask
    All reasons to refuse him;
But what she meets and what she fears
Are less than are the downward years,
Drawn slowly to the foamless weirs
    Of age, were she to lose him.

Between a blurred sagacity
    That once had power to sound him,
And Love, that will not let him be
    The Judas that she found him,
Her pride assuages her almost,
As if it were alone the cost.—
He sees that he will not be lost,
    And waits and looks around him.

A sense of ocean and old trees
    Envelops and allures him;
Tradition, touching all he sees,
    Beguiles and reassures him;
And all her doubts of what he says
Are dimmed with what she knows of days—
Till even prejudice delays
    And fades, and she secures him.

The falling leaf inaugurates
    The reign of her confusion;
The pounding wave reverberates
    The dirge of her illusion;
And home, where passion lived and died,
Becomes a place where she can hide,

While all the town and harbour side
　　Vibrate with her seclusion.

We tell you, tapping on our brows,
　　The story as it should be—
As if the story of a house
　　Were told, or ever could be;
We'll have no kindly veil between
Her visions and those we have seen—
As if we guessed what hers have been,
　　Or what they are or would be.

Meanwhile we do no harm; for they
　　That with a god have striven,
Not hearing much of what we say,
　　Take what the god has given;
Though like waves breaking it may be,
Or like a changed familiar tree,
Or like a stairway to the sea
　　Where down the blind are driven.

## Uncle Ananias

His words were magic and his heart was true,
　　And everywhere he wandered he was blessed.
Out of all ancient men my childhood knew
　　I choose him and I mark him for the best.
Of all authoritative liars, too,
　　I crown him loveliest.

How fondly I remember the delight
　　That always glorified him in the spring;
The joyous courage and the benedight
　　Profusion of his faith in everything!
He was a good old man, and it was right
　　That he should have his fling.

And often, underneath the apple-trees,
　　When we surprised him in the summer-time,

With what superb magnificence and ease
  He sinned enough to make the day sublime!
And if he liked us there about his knees,
  Truly it was no crime.

All summer long we loved him for the same
  Perennial inspiration of his lies;
And when the russet wealth of autumn came,
  There flew but fairer visions to our eyes—
Multiple, tropical, winged with a feathery flame,
  Like birds of paradise.

So to the sheltered end of many a year
  He charmed the seasons out with pageantry
Wearing upon his forehead, with no fear,
  The laurel of approved iniquity.
And every child who knew him, far or near,
  Did love him faithfully.

## The Master

SUPPOSED TO HAVE BEEN WRITTEN
NOT LONG AFTER THE CIVIL WAR

A flying word from here and there
Had sown the name at which we sneered,
But soon the name was everywhere,
To be reviled and then revered:
A presence to be loved and feared,
We cannot hide it, or deny
That we, the gentlemen who jeered,
May be forgotten by and by.

He came when days were perilous
And hearts of men were sore beguiled;
And having made his note of us,
He pondered and was reconciled.
Was ever master yet so mild
As he, and so untamable?

We doubted, even when he smiled,
Not knowing what he knew so well.

He knew that undeceiving fate
Would shame us whom he served unsought;
He knew that he must wince and wait—
The jest of those for whom he fought;
He knew devoutly what he thought
Of us and of our ridicule;
He knew that we must all be taught
Like little children in a school.

We gave a glamour to the task
That he encountered and saw through,
But little of us did he ask,
And little did we ever do.
And what appears if we review
The season when we railed and chaffed?
It is the face of one who knew
That we were learning while we laughed.

The face that in our vision feels
Again the venom that we flung,
Transfigured to the world reveals
The vigilance to which we clung.
Shrewd, hallowed, harassed, and among
The mysteries that are untold,
The face we see was never young,
Nor could it ever have been old.

For he, to whom we had applied
Our shopman's test of age and worth,
Was elemental when he died,
As he was ancient at his birth:
The saddest among kings of earth,
Bowed with a galling crown, this man
Met rancor with a cryptic mirth,
Laconic—and Olympian.

The love, the grandeur, and the fame
Are bounded by the world alone;
The calm, the smoldering, and the flame
Of awful patience were his own:
With him they are forever flown
Past all our fond self-shadowings,
Wherewith we cumber the Unknown
As with inept Icarian wings.

For we were not as other men:
'Twas ours to soar and his to see.
But we are coming down again,
And we shall come down pleasantly;
Nor shall we longer disagree
On what it is to be sublime,
But flourish in our perigee
And have one Titan at a time.


## Credo

I cannot find my way: there is no star
In all the shrouded heavens anywhere;
And there is not a whisper in the air
Of any living voice but one so far
That I can hear it only as a bar
Of lost, imperial music, played when fair
And angel fingers wove, and unaware,
Dead leaves to garlands where no roses are.

No, there is not a glimmer, nor a call,
For one that welcomes, welcomes when he fears,
The black and awful chaos of the night;
But through it all,—above, beyond it all—
I know the far-sent message of the years,
I feel the coming glory of the Light!

AMY LOWELL                                          1874–1925

### Madonna of the Evening Flowers

All day long I have been working,
Now I am tired.
I call: "Where are you?"
But there is only the oak tree rustling in the wind.
The house is very quiet,
The sun shines in on your books,
On your scissors and thimble just put down,
But you are not there.
Suddenly I am lonely:
Where are you?
I go about searching.

Then I see you,
Standing under a spire of pale blue larkspur,
With a basket of roses on your arm.
You are cool, like silver,
And you smile.
I think the Canterbury bells are playing little tunes,
You tell me that the peonies need spraying,
That the columbines have overrun all bounds,
That the pyrus japonica should be cut back and rounded.
You tell me these things.
But I look at you, heart of silver,
White heart-flame of polished silver,
Burning beneath the blue steeples of the larkspur,
And I long to kneel instantly at your feet,
While all about us peal the loud, sweet, Te Deums of the
    Canterbury bells.

# ROBERT FROST                                    1875–

### *Mowing*

There was never a sound beside the wood but one,
And that was my long scythe whispering to the ground.
What was it it whispered? I knew not well myself;
Perhaps it was something about the heat of the sun,
Something, perhaps, about the lack of sound—
And that was why it whispered and did not speak.
It was no dream of the gift of idle hours,
Or easy gold at the hand of fay or elf:
Anything more than the truth would have seemed too weak
To the earnest love that laid the swale in rows,
Not without feeble-pointed spikes of flowers
(Pale orchises), and scared a bright green snake.
The fact is the sweetest dream that labor knows.
My long scythe whispered and left the hay to rake.

### *The Death of the Hired Man*

Mary sat musing on the lamp-flame at the table
Waiting for Warren. When she heard his step,
She ran on tip-toe down the darkened passage
To meet him in the doorway with the news
And put him on his guard. "Silas is back."
She pushed him outward with her through the door
And shut it after her. "Be kind," she said.
She took the market things from Warren's arms
And set them on the porch, then drew him down
To sit beside her on the wooden steps.

Additional poems by this author may be found in *The Pocket Book of Robert Frost's Poems.*

"When was I ever anything but kind to him?
But I'll not have the fellow back," he said.
"I told him so last haying, didn't I?
'If he left then,' I said, 'that ended it.'
What good is he? Who else will harbour him
And his age for the little he can do?
What help he is there's no depending on.
Off he goes always when I need him most.
'He thinks he ought to earn a little pay,
Enough at least to buy tobacco with,
So he won't have to beg and be beholden.'
'All right,' I say, 'I can't afford to pay
Any fixed wages, though I wish I could.'
'Someone else can.' 'Then someone else will have to.'
I shouldn't mind his bettering himself
If that was what it was. You can be certain,
When he begins like that, there's someone at him
Trying to coax him off with pocket-money,—
In haying time, when any help is scarce.
In winter he comes back to us. I'm done."

"Sh! not so loud: he'll hear you," Mary said.

"I want him to: he'll have to soon or late."

"He's worn out. He's asleep beside the stove.
When I came up from Rowe's I found him here,
Huddled against the barn-door fast asleep,
A miserable sight, and frightening, too—
You needn't smile—I didn't recognise him—
I wasn't looking for him—and he's changed.
Wait till you see."

"Where did you say he'd been?"

"He didn't say. I dragged him to the house,
And gave him tea and tried to make him smoke.
I tried to make him talk about his travels.
Nothing would do: he just kept nodding off."

"What did he say? Did he say anything?"

"But little."

    "Anything? Mary, confess
He said he'd come to ditch the meadow for me."

"Warren!"

    "But did he? I just want to know."

"Of course he did. What would you have him say?
Surely you wouldn't grudge the poor old man
Some humble way to save his self-respect.
He added, if you really care to know,
He meant to clear the upper pasture, too.
That sounds like something you have heard before?
Warren, I wish you could have heard the way
He jumbled everything. I stopped to look
Two or three times—he made me feel so queer—
To see if he was talking in his sleep.
He ran on Harold Wilson—you remember—
The boy you had in haying four years since.
He's finished school, and teaching in his college.
Silas declares you'll have to get him back.
He says they two will make a team for work:
Between them they will lay this farm as smooth!
The way he mixed that in with other things.
He thinks young Wilson a likely lad, though daft
On education—you know how they fought
All through July under the blazing sun,
Silas up on the cart to build the load,
Harold along beside to pitch it on."

"Yes, I took care to keep well out of earshot."

"Well, those days trouble Silas like a dream.
You wouldn't think they would. How some things linger!
Harold's young college boy's assurance piqued him.
After so many years he still keeps finding
Good arguments he sees he might have used.
I sympathise. I know just how it feels
To think of the right thing to say too late.
Harold's associated in his mind with Latin.
He asked me what I thought of Harold's saying
He studied Latin like the violin
Because he liked it—that an argument!
He said he couldn't make the boy believe
He could find water with a hazel prong—
Which showed how much good school had ever done him.
He wanted to go over that. But most of all
He thinks if he could have another chance
To teach him how to build a load of hay—"

"I know, that's Silas' one accomplishment.
He bundles every forkful in its place,
And tags and numbers it for future reference,
So he can find and easily dislodge it
In the unloading. Silas does that well.
He takes it out in bunches like big birds' nests.
You never see him standing on the hay
He's trying to lift, straining to lift himself."

"He thinks if he could teach him that, he'd be
Some good perhaps to someone in the world.
He hates to see a boy the fool of books.
Poor Silas, so concerned for other folk,
And nothing to look backward to with pride,
And nothing to look forward to with hope,
So now and never any different."

Part of a moon was falling down the west,
Dragging the whole sky with it to the hills.
Its light poured softly in her lap. She saw
And spread her apron to it. She put out her hand
Among the harp-like morning-glory strings,
Taut with the dew from garden bed to eaves,
As if she played unheard the tenderness
That wrought on him beside her in the night.
"Warren," she said, "he has come home to die:
You needn't be afraid he'll leave you this time."

"Home," he mocked gently.

　　　"Yes, what else but home?
It all depends on what you mean by home.
Of course he's nothing to us, any more
Than was the hound that came a stranger to us
Out of the woods, worn out upon the trail."

"Home is the place where, when you have to go there,
They have to take you in."

　　　"I should have called it
Something you somehow haven't to deserve."

Warren leaned out and took a step or two,
Picked up a little stick, and brought it back
And broke it in his hand and tossed it by.
"Silas has better claim on us, you think,
Than on his brother? Thirteen little miles
As the road winds would bring him to his door.
Silas has walked that far no doubt to-day.
Why didn't he go there? His brother's rich,
A somebody—director in the bank."

"He never told us that."

"We knew it though."

"I think his brother ought to help, of course,
I'll see to that if there is need. He ought of right
To take him in, and might be willing to—
He may be better than appearances.
But have some pity on Silas. Do you think
If he'd had any pride in claiming kin
Or anything he looked for from his brother,
He'd keep so still about him all this time?"

"I wonder what's between them."

   "I can tell you.
Silas is what he is—we wouldn't mind him—
But just the kind that kinsfolk can't abide.
He never did a thing so very bad.
He don't know why he isn't quite as good
As anyone. He won't be made ashamed
To please his brother, worthless though he is."

"*I* can't think Si ever hurt anyone."

"No, but he hurt my heart the way he lay
And rolled his old head on that sharp-edged chair-back.
He wouldn't let me put him on the lounge.
You must go in and see what you can do.
I made the bed up for him there to-night.
You'll be surprised at him—how much he's broken.
His working days are done; I'm sure of it."

"I'd not be in a hurry to say that."

"I haven't been. Go, look, see for yourself.
But, Warren, please remember how it is:
He's come to help you ditch the meadow.

He has a plan. You mustn't laugh at him.
He may not speak of it, and then he may.
I'll sit and see if that small sailing cloud
Will hit or miss the moon."

It hit the moon.
Then there were three there, making a dim row,
The moon, the little silver cloud, and she.

Warren returned—too soon, it seemed to her,
Slipped to her side, caught up her hand and waited.

"Warren," she questioned.

"Dead," was all he answered.

## The Runaway

Once, when the snow of the year was beginning to fall,
We stopped by a mountain pasture to say "Whose colt?"
A little Morgan had one forefoot on the wall,
The other curled at his breast. He dipped his head
And snorted at us. And then he had to bolt.
We heard the miniature thunder where he fled
And we saw him, or thought we saw him, dim and grey,
Like a shadow against the curtain of falling flakes.
"I think the little fellow's afraid of the snow.
He isn't winter-broken. It isn't play
With the little fellow at all. He's running away.
I doubt if even his mother could tell him, 'Sakes,
It's only weather.' He'd think she didn't know!
Where is his mother? He can't be out alone."
And now he comes again with a clatter of stone
And mounts the wall again with whited eyes
And all his tail that isn't hair up straight.
He shudders his coat as if to throw off flies.
"Whoever it is that leaves him out so late,
When other creatures have gone to stall and bin,
Ought to be told to come and take him in."

## Hyla Brook

By June our brook's run out of song and speed.
Sought for much after that, it will be found
Either to have gone groping underground
(And taken with it all the Hyla breed
That shouted in the mist a month ago,
Like ghost of sleigh-bells in a ghost of snow)—
Or flourished and come up in jewel-weed,
Weak foliage that is blown upon and bent
Even against the way its waters went.
Its bed is left a faded paper sheet
Of dead leaves stuck together by the heat—
A brook to none but who remember long.
This as it will be seen is other far
Than with brooks taken otherwhere in song.
We love the things we love for what they are.

## The Telephone

"When I was just as far as I could walk
From here to-day,
There was an hour
All still
When leaning with my head against a flower
I heard you talk.
Don't say I didn't, for I heard you say—
You spoke from that flower on the window sill—
Do you remember what it was you said?"

"First tell me what it was you thought you heard."

"Having found the flower and driven a bee away,
I leaned my head,
And holding by the stalk,
I listened and I thought I caught the word—

What was it? Did you call me by my name?
Or did you say—
Someone said 'Come'—I heard it as I bowed."

"I may have thought as much, but not aloud."

"Well, so I came."

## Choose Something Like a Star

O Star (the fairest one in sight),
We grant your loftiness the right
To some obscurity of cloud—
It will not do to say of night,
Since dark is what brings out your light.
Some mystery becomes the proud.
But to be wholly taciturn
In your reserve is not allowed.
Say something to us we can learn
By heart and when alone repeat.
Say something! And it says "I burn."
But say with what degree of heat.
Talk Fahrenheit, talk Centigrade.
Use language we can comprehend.
Tell us what elements you blend.
It gives us strangely little aid,
But does tell something in the end.
And steadfast as Keats' Eremite,
Not even stooping from its sphere,
It asks a little of us here.
It asks of us a certain height,
So when at times the mob is swayed
To carry praise or blame too far,
We may choose something like a star
To stay our minds on and be staid.

CARL SANDBURG                                    1878–

*Upstream*

The strong men keep coming on,
They go down shot, hanged, sick, broken.
They live on fighting, singing, lucky as plungers.
The strong mothers pulling them on . . .
The strong mothers pulling them from a dark sea, a great
    prairie, a long mountain.
Call hallelujah, call amen, call deep thanks.
The strong men keep coming on.

*Prayers of Steel*

Lay me on an anvil, O God.
Beat me and hammer me into a crowbar.
Let me pry loose old walls.
Let me lift and loosen old foundations.

Lay me on an anvil, O God.
Beat me and hammer me into a steel spike.
Drive me into the girders that hold a skyscraper together.
Take red-hot rivets and fasten me into the central girders.
Let me be the great nail holding a skyscraper through blue
    nights into white stars.

VACHEL LINDSAY                            1879–1931

### The Eagle That Is Forgotten

JOHN P. ALTGELD. BORN DECEMBER 30, 1847; DIED MARCH 12, 1902

Sleep softly . . . eagle forgotten . . . under the stone,
Time has its way with you there, and the clay has its own.
"We have buried him now," thought your foes, and in secret
    rejoiced.
They made a brave show of their mourning, their hatred un-
    voiced.
They had snarled at you, barked at you, foamed at you, day
    after day,
Now you were ended. They praised you, . . . and laid you
    away.

The others that mourned you in silence and terror and truth,
The widow bereft of her pittance, the boy without youth,
The mocked and the scorned and the wounded, the lame and
    the poor
That should have remembered forever, . . . remember no
    more.

Where are those lovers of yours, on what name do they call
The lost, that in armies wept over your funeral pall?
They call on the names of a hundred high-valiant ones,
A hundred white eagles have risen, the sons of your sons,
The zeal in their wings is a zeal that your dreaming began,
The valor that wore out your soul in the service of man.

Sleep softly, . . . eagle forgotten, . . . under the stone,
Time has its way with you there, and the clay has its own.

Sleep on, O brave hearted, O wise man, that kindled the
    flame—
To live in mankind is far more than to live in a name,
To live in mankind, far, far more . . . than to live in a name.


## The Broncho That Would Not Be Broken

A little colt—broncho, loaned to the farm
To be broken in time without fury or harm,
Yet black crows flew past you, shouting alarm,
Calling "Beware," with lugubrious singing . . .
The butterflies there in the bush were romancing,
The smell of the grass caught your soul in a trance,
So why be a-fearing the spurs and the traces,
O broncho that would not be broken of dancing?

You were born with the pride of the lords great and olden
Who danced, through the ages, in corridors golden.
In all the wide farm-place the person most human.
You spoke out so plainly with squealing and capering,
With whinnying, snorting contorting and prancing,
As you dodged your pursuers, looking askance,
With Greek-footed figures, and Parthenon paces,
O broncho that would not be broken of dancing.

The grasshoppers cheered. "Keep whirling," they said.
The insolent sparrows called from the shed
"If men will not laugh, make them wish they were dead."
But arch were your thoughts, all malice displacing,
Though the horse-killers came, with snake-whips advancing.
You bantered and cantered away your last chance.
And they scourged you, with Hell in their speech and their
    faces,
O broncho that would not be broken of dancing.

"Nobody cares for you," rattled the crows,
As you dragged the whole reaper, next day, down the rows.
The three mules held back, yet you danced on your toes.
You pulled like a racer, and kept the mules chasing.
You tangled the harness with bright eyes side-glancing,
While the drunk driver bled you—a pole for a lance—
And the giant mules bit at you—keeping their places.
O broncho that would not be broken of dancing.

In that last afternoon your boyish heart broke.
The hot wind came down like a sledge-hammer stroke.
The blood-sucking flies to a rare feast awoke.
And they searched out your wounds, your death-warrant
    tracing.
And the merciful men, their religion enhancing,
Stopped the red reaper, to give you a chance.
Then you died on the prairie, and scorned all disgraces,
O broncho that would not be broken of dancing.


WALLACE STEVENS                              1879–

### To the One of Fictive Music

Sister and mother and diviner love,
And of the sisterhood of the living dead
Most near, most clear, and of the clearest bloom,
And of the fragrant mothers the most dear
And queen, and of diviner love the day
And flame and summer and sweet fire, no thread
Of cloudy silver sprinkles in your gown
Its venom of renown, and on your head
No crown is simpler than the simple hair.

Now, of the music summoned by the birth
That separates us from the wind and sea,

Yet leaves us in them, until earth becomes,
By being so much of the things we are,
Gross effigy and simulacrum, none
Gives motion to perfection more serene
Than yours, out of our imperfections wrought,
Most rare, or ever of more kindred air
In the laborious weaving that you wear.

For so retentive of themselves are men
That music is intensest which proclaims
The near, the clear, and vaunts the clearest bloom,
And of all vigils musing the obscure,
That apprehends the most which sees and names,
As in your name, an image that is sure,
Among the arrant spices of the sun,
O bough and bush and scented vine, in whom
We give ourselves our likest issuance.

Yet not too like, yet not so like to be
Too near, too clear, saving a little to endow
Our feigning with the strange unlike, whence springs
The difference that heavenly pity brings.
For this, musician, in your girdle fixed
Bear other perfumes. On your pale head wear
A band entwining, set with fatal stones.
Unreal, give back to us what once you gave:
The imagination that we spurned and crave.

# SARA TEASDALE                    1884–1933

## Wisdom

It was a night of early spring,
　　The winter-sleep was scarcely broken;
Around us shadows and the wind
　　Listened for what was never spoken.

Though half a score of years are gone,
　　Spring comes as sharply now as then—
But if we had it all to do
　　It would be done the same again.

It was a spring that never came;
　　But we have lived enough to know
That what we never have, remains;
　　It is the things we have that go.

## Let It Be Forgotten

Let it be forgotten, as a flower is forgotten,
　　Forgotten as a fire that once was singing gold,
Let it be forgotten for ever and ever,
　　Time is a kind friend, he will make us old.

If anyone asks, say it was forgotten
　　Long and long ago,
As a flower, as a fire, as a hushed footfall
　　In a long-forgotten snow.

## ELINOR WYLIE                                    1885–1928

### *Winter Sleep*

When against earth a wooden heel
Clicks as loud as stone and steel,
When snow turns flour instead of flakes,
And frost bakes clay as fire bakes,
When the hard-bitten fields at last
Crack like iron flawed in the cast,
When the world is wicked and cross and old,
I long to be quit of the cruel cold.

Little birds like bubbles of glass
Fly to other Americas,
Birds as bright as sparkles of wine
Fly in the night to the Argentine,
Birds of azure and flame-birds go
To the tropical Gulf of Mexico:
They chase the sun, they follow the heat,
It is sweet in their bones, O sweet, sweet, sweet!
It's not with them that I'd love to be,
But under the roots of the balsam tree.

Just as the spiniest chestnut-burr
Is lined within with the finest fur,
So the stony-walled, snow-roofed house
Of every squirrel and mole and mouse
Is lined with thistledown, sea-gull's feather,
Velvet mullein-leaf, heaped together
With balsam and juniper, dry and curled,
Sweeter than anything else in the world.
O what a warm and darksome nest
Where the wildest things are hidden to rest!
It's there that I'd love to lie and sleep,
Soft, soft, soft, and deep, deep, deep!

JEAN STARR UNTERMEYER          1886–

*Autumn*

TO MY MOTHER

How memory cuts away the years,
And how clean the picture comes
Of autumn days, brisk and busy;
Charged with keen sunshine.
And you, stirred with activity,
The spirit of those energetic days.

There was our back-yard,
So plain and stripped of green,
With even the weeds carefully pulled away
From the crooked red bricks that made the walk,
And the earth on either side so black.

Autumn and dead leaves burning in the sharp air.
And winter comforts coming in like a pageant.
I shall not forget them:—
Great jars pompous with the raw green of pickles,
Standing in a solemn row across the back of the porch,
Exhaling the pungent dill;
And in the very center of the yard,
You, tending the great catsup kettle of gleaming copper,
Where fat, red tomatoes bobbed up and down
Like jolly monks in a drunken dance.
And there were bland banks of cabbages that came by the
       wagon-load,
Soon to be cut into delicate ribbons
Only to be crushed by the heavy, wooden stompers.
Such feathery whiteness—to come to kraut!
And after, there were grapes that hid their brightness under
       a gray dust,
Then gushed thrilling, purple blood over the fire;

And enameled crab-apples that tricked with their fragrance
But were bitter to taste.
And there were spicy plums and ill-shaped quinces,
And long string beans floating in pans of clear water
Like slim, green fishes.
And there was fish itself,
Salted, silver herring from the city. . . .

And you moved among these mysteries,
Absorbed and smiling and sure;
Stirring, tasting, measuring,
With the precision of a ritual.
I like to think of you in your years of power—
You, now so shaken and so powerless—
High priestess of your home.

## Creative Word

In the Beginning was the Word
But the Word had to be heard.
The silence had to be broken,
The Word had to be spoken,
Before chaotic night
Resolved to ordered light.

Before the desert bed
Yielded the rose's head
The Word had to be said.

Before Eve was unbound
From Adam's lateral wound,
The Word had to sound.

As truth is true alway,
Imperative today,
There is the Word to say.

# H. D. (HILDA DOOLITTLE)                    1886-

## The Garden

### I

You are clear,
O rose, cut in rock.

I could scrape the colour
From the petals,
Like spilt dye from a rock.

If I could break you
I could break a tree.

If I could stir
I could break a tree,
I could break you.

### II

O wind, rend open the heat,
Cut apart the heat,
Slit it to tatters.

Fruit cannot drop
Through this thick air;
Fruit cannot fall into heat
That presses up and blunts
The points of pears,
And rounds grapes.

Cut the heat:
Plough through it,
Turning it on either side
Of your path.

## Lethe

Nor skin nor hide nor fleece
    Shall cover you,
Nor curtain of crimson nor fine
Shelter of cedar-wood be over you,
        Nor the fir-tree
        Nor the pine.

Nor sight of whin nor gorse
        Nor river-yew,
        Nor fragrance of flowering bush,
Nor wailing of reed-bird to waken you.
        Nor of linnet
        Nor of thrush.

Nor word nor touch nor sight
        Of lover, you
Shall long through the night but for this:
The roll of the full tide to cover you
        Without question,
        Without kiss.

# WILLIAM ROSE BENÉT 1886–

### The Fawn in the Snow

The brown-dappled fawn
Bereft of the doe
Shivers in blue shadow
Of the glaring snow,

His whole world bright
As a jewel, and hard,
Diamond white,
Turquoise barred.

The trees are black,
Their needles gold,
Their boughs crack
In the keen cold.

The brown-dappled fawn
Bereft of the doe
Trembles and shudders
At the bright snow.

The air whets
The warm throat,
The frost frets
At the smooth coat.

Brown agate eyes
Opened round
Agonize
At the cold ground,

At the cold heaven
Enameled pale,
At the earth shriven
By the snowy gale,

At magic glitter
Burning to blind,
At beauty bitter
As an almond rind.

Fawn, fawn,
Seek for your south,
For kind dawn
With her cool mouth,

For green sod
With gold and blue
Dappled, as God
Has dappled you,

For slumbrous ease,
Firm turf to run
Through fruited trees
Into full sun!

The shivering fawn
Paws at the snow.
South and dawn
Lie below;

Richness and mirth,
Dearth forgiven,
A happy earth,
A warm heaven.

> The sleet streams;
> The snow flies;
> The fawn dreams
> With wide brown eyes.

# JOHN HALL WHEELOCK                    1886–

## *Triumph of Love*

I shake my hair in the wind of morning
  For the joy within me that knows no bounds,
I echo backward the vibrant beauty
  Wherewith heaven's hollow lute resounds.

I shed my song on the feet of all men,
  On the feet of all shed out like wine,
On the whole and the hurt I shed my bounty,
  The beauty within me that is not mine.

Turn not away from my song, nor scorn me,
  Who bear the secret that holds the sky
And the stars together, but know within me
  There speaks another more wise than I.

Nor spurn me here from your heart, to hate me!
  Yet hate me here if you will—not so
Myself you hate, but the Love within me
  That loves you, whether you would or no.

Here love returns with love to the lover,
  And beauty unto the heart thereof,
And hatred unto the heart of the hater,
  Whether he would or no, with love!

MARIANNE MOORE                                1887–

*The Fish*

Wade
through black jade
    Of the crow-blue mussel shells, one keeps
      adjusting the ash heaps;
    opening and shutting itself like

an
injured fan.
    The barnacles which encrust the side
      of the wave, cannot hide
    there for the submerged shafts of the

sun,
split like spun
    glass, move themselves with spotlight swiftness
      into the crevices—
    in and out, illuminating

the
turquoise sea
    of bodies. The water drives a wedge
      of iron through the iron edge
    of the cliff, whereupon the stars,

pink
rice grains, ink
    bespattered jelly-fish, crabs like green
      lilies and submarine
    toadstools, slide each on the other.

All
external
    marks of abuse are present on this
        defiant edifice—
    all the physical features of

ac-
cident—lack
    of cornice, dynamite grooves, burns and
        hatchet strokes, these things stand
    out on it; the chasm side is

dead.
Repeated
    evidence has proved that it can live
        on what cannot revive
    its youth. The sea grows old in it.


## ROBINSON JEFFERS                    1887–

### *Hurt Hawks*

The broken pillar of the wing jags from the clotted shoulder,
The wing trails like a banner in defeat,
No more to use the sky forever but live with famine
And pain a few days: cat nor coyote
Will shorten the week of waiting for death, there is game
        without talons.

He stands under the oak-bush and waits
The lame feet of salvation; at night he remembers freedom
And flies in a dream, the dawns ruin it.
He is strong and pain is worse to the strong, incapacity is
        worse.
The curs of the day come and torment him

At distance, no one but death the redeemer will humble that
   head,
The intrepid readiness, the terrible eyes.
The wild God of the world is sometimes merciful to those
That ask mercy, not often to the arrogant.
You do not know him, you communal people, or you have for-
   gotten him;
Intemperate and savage, the hawk remembers him;
Beautiful and wild, the hawks, and men that are dying re-
   member him.

⁂

I'd sooner, except the penalties, kill a man than a hawk; but
   the great redtail
Had nothing left but unable misery
From the bone too shattered for mending, the wing that
   trailed under his talons when he moved.
We had fed him six weeks, I gave him freedom,
He wandered over the foreland hill and returned in the eve-
   ning, asking for death,
Not like a beggar, still eyed with the old
Implacable arrogance. I gave him the lead gift in the twilight.
                              What fell was relaxed,
Owl-downy, soft feminine feathers; but what
Soared: the fierce rush: the night-herons by the flooded river
   cried fear at its rising
Before it was quite unsheathed from reality.

## JOHN CROWE RANSOM                    1888–

### Bells for John Whiteside's Daughter

There was such speed in her little body,
And such lightness in her footfall,
It is no wonder that her brown study
Astonishes us all.

Her wars were bruited in our high window.
We looked among orchard trees and beyond,
Where she took arms against her shadow,
Or harried unto the pond

The lazy geese, like a snow cloud
Dripping their snow on the green grass,
Tricking and stopping, sleepy and proud,
Who cried in goose, Alas,

For the tireless heart within the little
Lady with rod that made them rise
From their noon apple-dreams, and scuttle
Goose-fashion under the skies!

But now go the bells, and we are ready;
In one house we are sternly stopped
To say we are vexed at her brown study,
Lying so primly propped.

CONRAD AIKEN                              1889–

## The Quarrel

Suddenly, after the quarrel, while we waited,
Disheartened, silent, with downcast looks, nor stirred
Eyelid nor finger, hopeless both, yet hoping
Against all hope to unsay the sundering word:

While all the room's stillness deepened, deepened about us,
And each of us crept his thought's way to discover
How, with as little sound as the fall of a leaf,
The shadow had fallen, and lover quarreled with lover;

And while, in the quiet, I marveled—alas, alas—
At your deep beauty, your tragic beauty, torn
As the pale flower is torn by the wanton sparrow—
This beauty, pitied and loved, and now forsworn;

It was then, when the instant darkened to its darkest,—
When faith was lost with hope, and the rain conspired
To strike its gray arpeggios against our heartstrings,—
When love no longer dared, and scarcely desired:

It was then that suddenly, in the neighbor's room,
The music started: that brave quartette of strings
Breaking out of the stillness, as out of our stillness,
Like the indomitable heart of life that sings

When all is lost; and startled from our sorrow,
Tranced from our grief by that diviner grief,
We raised remembering eyes, each looked at other,
Blinded with tears of joy; and another leaf

Fell silently as that first; and in the instant
The shadow had gone, our quarrel became absurd;
And we rose, to the angelic voices of the music,
And I touched your hand, and we kissed, without a word.

## EDNA ST. VINCENT MILLAY                    1892–

### Pity Me Not

Pity me not because the light of day
At close of day no longer walks the sky;
Pity me not for beauties passed away
From field and thicket as the year goes by;
Pity me not the waning of the moon,
Nor that the ebbing tide goes out to sea,
Nor that a man's desire is hushed so soon,
And you no longer look with love on me.

This have I known always: love is no more
Than the wide blossom which the wind assails;
Than the great tide that treads the shifting shore,
Strewing fresh wreckage gathered in the gales.
Pity me that the heart is slow to learn
What the swift mind beholds at every turn.

### Dirge without Music

I am not resigned to the shutting away of loving hearts in the
    hard ground.
So it is, and so it will be, for so it has been, time out of mind:
Into the darkness they go, the wise and the lovely. Crowned
With lilies and with laurel they go; but I am not resigned.

Lovers and thinkers, into the earth with you.
Be one with the dull, the indiscriminate dust.
A fragment of what you felt, of what you knew,
A formula, a phrase remains,—but the best is lost.

The answers quick and keen, the honest look, the laughter,
    the love,—
They are gone. They have gone to feed the roses. Elegant and
    curled

Is the blossom. Fragrant is the blossom. I know. But I do not
    approve.
More precious was the light in your eyes than all the roses in
    the world.

Down, down, down into the darkness of the grave
Gently they go, the beautiful, the tender, the kind;
Quietly they go, the intelligent, the witty, the brave.
I know. But I do not approve. And I am not resigned.

## ARCHIBALD MACLEISH                                    1892–

### You, Andrew Marvell

And here face down beneath the sun
And here upon earth's noonward height
To feel the always coming on
The always rising of the night

To feel creep up the curving east
The earthly chill of dusk and slow
Upon those under lands the vast
And ever-climbing shadow grow

And strange at Ecbatan the trees
Take leaf by leaf the evening strange
The flooding dark about their knees
The mountains over Persia change

And now at Kermanshah the gate
Dark empty and the withered grass
And through the twilight now the late
Few travelers in the westward pass

And Baghdad darken and the bridge
Across the silent river gone
And through Arabia the edge
Of evening widen and steal on

And deepen on Palmyra's street
The wheel rut in the ruined stone
And Lebanon fade out and Crete
High through the clouds and overblown

And over Sicily the air
Still flashing with the landward gulls
And loom and slowly disappear
The sails above the shadowy hulls

And Spain go under and the shore
Of Africa the gilded sand
And evening vanish and no more
The low pale light across that land

Nor now the long light on the sea—
And here face downward in the sun
To feel how swift how secretly
The shadow of the night comes on. . . .

## The End of the World

Quite unexpectedly as Vasserot
The armless ambidextrian was lighting
A match between his great and second toe
And Ralph the lion was engaged in biting
The neck of Madame Sossman while the drum
Pointed, and Terry was about to cough
In waltz-time swinging Jocko by the thumb—
Quite unexpectedly the top blew off:

And there, there overhead, there, there, hung over
Those thousands of white faces, those dazed eyes,
There in the starless dark, the poise, the hover,
There with vast wings across the canceled skies,
There in the sudden blackness the black pall
Of nothing, nothing, nothing—nothing at all.

E. E. CUMMINGS                                    1894–

### Somewhere I Have Never Travelled

somewhere i have never travelled, gladly beyond
any experience, your eyes have their silence:
in your most frail gesture are things which enclose me,
or which i cannot touch because they are too near

your slightest look easily will unclose me
though i have closed myself as fingers,
you open always petal by petal myself as Spring opens
(touching skilfully, mysteriously) her first rose

or if your wish be to close me, i and
my life will shut very beautifully, suddenly,
as when the heart of this flower imagines
the snow carefully everywhere descending;

nothing which we are to perceive in this world equals
the power of your intense fragility: whose texture
compels me with the color of its countries,
rendering death and forever with each breathing

(i do not know what it is about you that closes
and opens; only something in me understands
the voice of your eyes is deeper than all roses)
nobody, not even the rain, has such small hands

# HORACE GREGORY                    1898–

## *Ask No Return*

Ask no return for love that's given
embracing mistress, wife or friend,
                          ask no return:
on this deep earth or in pale heaven,
awake and spend
hands, lips and eyes in love,
in darkness burn,
             the limbs entwined until the soul ascend.

Ask no return of seasons gone:
the fire of autumn and the first hour of spring,
the short bough blossoming
through city windows when night's done,
when fears adjourn
                     backward in memory where all loves end
in self again, again the inward tree
growing against the heart
and no heart free.
From love that sleeps behind each eye
in double symmetry
                    ask no return,
even in enmity, look! I shall take your hand;
nor can our limbs disjoin in separate ways again,
walking, even at night on foreign land
through houses open to the wind, through cold and rain,
waking alive, meet, kiss and understand.

# STEPHEN VINCENT BENÉT                    1898–1943

## American Names

I have fallen in love with American names,
The sharp names that never get fat,
The snakeskin-titles of mining-claims,
The plumed war-bonnet of Medicine Hat,
Tucson and Deadwood and Lost Mule Flat.

Seine and Piave are silver spoons,
But the spoonbowl-metal is thin and worn,
There are English counties like hunting-tunes
Played on the keys of a postboy's horn,
But I will remember where I was born.

I will remember Carquinez Straits,
Little French Lick and Lundy's Lane,
The Yankee ships and the Yankee dates
And the bullet-towns of Calamity Jane.
I will remember Skunktown Plain.

I will fall in love with a Salem tree
And a rawhide quirt from Santa Cruz,
I will get me a bottle of Boston sea
And a blue-gum nigger to sing me blues.
I am tired of loving a foreign muse.

Rue des Martyrs and Bleeding-Heart-Yard,
Senlis, Pisa, and Blindman's Oast,
It is a magic ghost you guard.
But I am sick for a newer ghost,
Harrisburg, Spartanburg, Painted Post.

Additional poems by this author may be found in *The Stephen Vincent Benét Pocket Book.*

Henry and John were never so,
And Henry and John were always right?
Granted, but when it was time to go
And the tea and the laurels had stood all night
Did they never watch for Nantucket Light?

I shall not rest quiet in Montparnasse.
I shall not lie easy at Winchelsea.
You may bury my body in Sussex grass,
You may bury my tongue at Champmédy.
I shall not be there. I shall rise and pass.
Bury my heart at Wounded Knee.

## Nightmare Number Three

We had expected everything but revolt
And I kind of wonder myself when they started thinking—
But there's no dice in that now.

                           I've heard fellows say
They must have planned it for years and maybe they did.
Looking back, you can find little incidents here and there,
Like the concrete-mixer in Jersey eating the wop
Or the roto press that printed "Fiddle-dee-dee!"
In a three-color process all over Senator Sloop,
Just as he was making a speech. The thing about that
Was, how could it walk upstairs? But it *was* upstairs,
Clicking and mumbling in the Senate Chamber.
They had to knock out the wall to take it away
And the wrecking-crew said it grinned.

                           It was only the best
Machines, of course, the superhuman machines,
The ones we'd built to be better than flesh and bone,
But the cars were in it, of course . . .

                           and they hunted us

Like rabbits through the cramped streets on that Bloody Mon-
    day,
The Madison Avenue busses leading the charge.
The busses were pretty bad—but I'll not forget
The smash of glass when the Duesenberg left the show-room
And pinned three brokers to the Racquet Club steps,
Or the long howl of the horns when they saw the men run,
When they saw them looking for holes in the solid ground . . .

I guess they were tired of being ridden in,
And stopped and started by pygmies for silly ends,
Of wrapping cheap cigarettes and bad chocolate bars,
Collecting nickels and waving platinum hair,
And letting six million people live in a town.
I guess it was that. I guess they got tired of us
And the whole smell of human hands.

                                    But it was a shock
To climb sixteen flights of stairs to Art Zuckow's office
(Nobody took the elevators twice)
And find him strangled to death in a nest of telephones,
The octopus-tendrils waving over his head,
And a sort of quiet humming filling the air . . .
Do they eat? . . . There was red . . . But I did not stop to
    look.
And it's lonely, here on the roof.
                            For a while I thought
That window-cleaner would make it, and keep me company.
But they got him with his own hoist at the sixteenth floor
And dragged him in with a squeal.
You see, they cooperate. Well, we taught them that,
And it's fair enough, I suppose. You see, we built them.
We taught them to think for themselves.
It was bound to come. You can see it was bound to come.
And it won't be so bad, in the country. I hate to think
Of the reapers, running wild in the Kansas fields,

And the transport planes like hawks on a chickenyard,
But the horses might help. We might make a deal with the
    horses.
At least you've more chance, out there.

                        And they need us too.
They're bound to realize that when they once calm down.
They'll need oil and spare parts and adjustments and tuning
    up.
Slaves? Well, in a way, you know, we were slaves before.
There won't be so much real difference—honest there won't.
(I wish I hadn't looked into that beauty-parlor
And seen what was happening there.
But those are female machines and a bit high-strung.)
Oh, we'll settle down. We'll arrange it. We'll compromise.
It wouldn't make sense to wipe out the whole human race.
Why, I bet if I went to my old Plymouth now
(Of course, you'd have to do it the tactful way)
And said, "Look here! Who got you the swell French horn?"
He wouldn't turn me over to those police cars.
At least I don't think he would.

                      Oh, it's going to be jake.
There won't be so much real difference—honest, there
    won't—
And I'd go down in a minute and take my chance—
I'm a good American and I always liked them—
Except for one small detail that bothers me
And that's the food proposition. Because you see,
The concrete-mixer may have made a mistake,
And it looks like just high spirits.
But, if it's got so they like the flavor . . . well . . .

HART CRANE                                    1899–1932

## Voyages: II

—And yet this great wing of eternity,
Of rimless floods, unfettered leewardings,
Samite sheeted and processioned where
Her undinal vast belly moonward bends,
Laughing the wrapt inflections of our love;

Take this Sea, whose diapason knells
On scrolls of silver snowy sentences,
The sceptered terror of whose sessions rends
As her demeanors motion well or ill,
All but the pieties of lovers' hands.

And onward, as bells off San Salvador
Salute the crocus lusters of the stars,
In these poinsettia meadows of her tides,—
Adagios of islands, O my Prodigal,
Complete the dark confessions her veins spell.

Mark how her turning shoulders wind the hours,
And hasten while her penniless rich palms
Pass superscription of bent foam and wave,—
Hasten, while they are true,—sleep, death, desire,
Close round one instant in one floating flower.

Bind us in time, O seasons clear, and awe.
O minstrel galleons of Carib fire,
Bequeath us to no earthly shore until
Is answered in the vortex of our grave
The seal's wide spindrift gaze toward paradise.

LÉONIE ADAMS                                    1899–

### Sundown

This is the time lean woods shall spend
A steeped-up twilight, and the pale evening drink,
And the perilous roe, the leaper to the west brink,
Trembling and bright, to the caverned cloud descend.

Now shall you see pent oak gone gusty and frantic,
Stooped with dry weeping, ruinously unloosing
The sparse disheveled leaf, or reared and tossing
A dreary scarecrow bough in funeral antic.

Aye, tatter you and rend,
Oak heart, to your profession mourning, not obscure
The outcome, not crepuscular, on the deep floor,
Sable and gold match lusters and contend.

And rags of shrouding will not muffle the slain.
This is the immortal extinction, the priceless wound
Not to be staunched; the live gold leaks beyond,
And matter's sanctified, dipped in a gold stain.

MERRILL MOORE                                                 1903–

## Warning to One

Death is the strongest of all living things
And when it happens do not look in the eyes
For a dead fire or a lack-luster there,
But listen for the words that fall from lips
Or do not fall. Silence is not death;
It merely means that the one who is conserving breath
Is not concerned with tattle and small quips.

Watch the quick fingers and the way they move
During unguarded moments—words of love
And love's caresses may be cold as ice
And cold the glitter of engagement rings;
Death is the sword that hangs on a single hair,
And that thin tenuous hair is no more than love
And yours is the silly head it hangs above.

KARL SHAPIRO                                                  1913–

## The Leg

Among the iodoform, in twilight-sleep,
*What have I lost?* he first inquires,
Peers in the middle distance where a pain,
Ghost of a nurse, hastily moves, and day,
Her blinding presence pressing in his eyes
And now his ears. They are handling him
With rubber hands. He wants to get up.

One day beside some flowers near his nose
He will be thinking, *When will I look at it?*
And pain, still in the middle distance, will reply
*At what?* and he will know it's gone,
O where! and begin to tremble and cry.
He will begin to cry as a child cries
Whose puppy is mangled under a screaming wheel.

Later, as if deliberately, his fingers
Begin to explore the stump. He learns a shape
That is comfortable and tucked in like a sock.
This has a sense of humor, this can despise
The finest surgical limb, the dignity of limping,
The nonsense of wheel-chairs. Now he smiles to the wall:
The amputation becomes an acquisition.

For the leg is wondering where he is (all is not lost)
And surely he has a duty to the leg;
He is its injury, the leg is his orphan,
He must cultivate the mind of the leg,
Pray for the part that is missing, pray for peace
In the image of man, pray, pray for its safety,
And after a little it will die quietly.

The body, what is it, Father, but a sign
To love the force that grows us, to give back
What in Thy palm is senselessness and mud?
Knead, knead the substance of our understanding
Which must be beautiful in flesh to walk,
That if Thou take me angrily in hand
And hurl me to the shark, I shall not die!

## MURIEL RUKEYSER                                    1913–

### Boy with His Hair Cut Short

Sunday shuts down on this twentieth-century evening.
The L passes. Twilight and bulb define
the brown room, the overstuffed plum sofa,
the boy, and the girl's thin hands above his head.
A neighbor radio sings stocks, news, serenade.

He sits at the table, head down, the young clear neck ex-
          posed,
watching the drugstore sign from the tail of his eye;
tattoo, neon, until the eye blears, while his
solicitous tall sister, simple in blue, bending
behind him, cuts his hair with her cheap shears.

The arrow's electric red always reaches its mark,
successful neon! He coughs, impressed by that precision.
His child's forehead, forever protected by his cap,
is bleached against the lamplight as he turns head
and steadies to let the snippets drop.

Erasing the failure of weeks with level fingers,
she sleeks the fine hair, combing: "You'll look fine tomorrow!
You'll surely find something, they can't keep turning you
          down;
the finest gentleman's not so trim as you!" Smiling, he raises
the adolescent forehead wrinkling ironic now.

He sees his decent suit laid out, new-pressed,
his carfare on the shelf. He lets his head fall, meeting
her earnest hopeless look, seeing the sharp blades splitting,
the darkened room, the impersonal sign, her motion,
the blue vein, bright on her temple, pitifully beating.

# ROBERT LOWELL                                    1917–

## *Mary Winslow*

Her Irish maids could never spoon out mush
Or orange-juice enough; the body cools
And smiles as a sick child
Who adds up figures, and a hush
Grips at the poised relations sipping sherry
And tracking up the carpets of her four
Room kingdom. On the rigid Charles, in snow,
Charon, the Lubber, clambers from his wherry,
And stops her hideous baby-squawks and yells,
Wit's clownish afterthought. Nothing will go
Again. Even the gelded picador
Baiting the twinned runt bulls
With walrus horns before the Spanish Belles
Is veiled with all the childish bibelots.

Mary Winslow is dead. Out on the Charles
The shells hold water and their oarblades drag,
Littered with captivated ducks, and now
The bell-rope in King's Chapel Tower unsnarls
And bells the bestial cow
From Boston Common; she is dead. But stop,
Neighbor, these pillows prop
Her that her terrified and child's cold eyes
Glass what they're not: our Copley ancestress,
Grandiloquent, square-jowled and worldly-wise,
A Cleopatra in her housewife's dress;
Nothing will go again. The bells cry: "Come,
Come home," the babbling Chapel belfry cries:
"Come, Mary Winslow, come: I bell thee home."

# INDEX

Authors' names are printed in CAPITALS AND SMALL
    CAPITALS
Titles of poems are printed in ordinary Upper and
    Lower Case
First lines of poems are printed in *Italics*

# BEST SELLERS

## GENUINE POCKET BOOK EDITIONS

*Are there any you have missed? Of the more than 500 POCKET BOOK titles that have been published to date, these are some outstanding favorites:*

SEPTEMBER, 1948